THE LAST YEARS OF A REBEL

Edith Sitwell on her seventy-fifth birthday, 1962

The Last Years of a Rebel

A Memoir of Edith Sitwell

ELIZABETH SALTER

THE BODLEY HEAD
LONDON · SYDNEY
TORONTO

ACKNOWLEDGEMENTS

My grateful thanks are due to the following people and organisations for their generous and helpful co-operation:

Miss Lorna Andrade; Miss Natalie Barney; the Baroness de Bosmolet; Mrs Bradley; Mr Hugh Burnett; Mr and Mrs Henry Cecil; Miss Lorna Coates; the Estate of M. Jean Cocteau; Mr. Robert Covington; Mr Noel Coward; Mr George Cukor; Mrs Veronica Gilliat; Mr Graham Greene; Mr Timothy Green; Mrs Allanah Harper; Miss Elizabeth Jenkins; Mr J. W. Lambert; Mr Lancelot Law Whyte; Miss Vivien Leigh; Mr Maurice Levinson; Mr Jack Lindsay; Mr W. McCann; Mrs Hazel Guggenheim McKinley; Miss Sylva Norman; Miss Marjorie Proops; Mr James Purdy; Mr Tom Rothfield; the Hon. Mrs Rosemary Russell; Mr Humphrey Searle; Mrs Constance Sitwell; Lord and Lady Snow; Mr Michael Stapleton; the Hon Mrs Sherman Stonor; Mme Choura Zaoussailoff Tchelitchew; Miss Alice B. Toklas; Sir William Walton; Mr Gordon Watson; Miss Margaret Witchell.

I should also like to express my gratitude to Sir Osbert Sitwell for his encouragement to me in writing this book, and to the Estate of Dame Edith Sitwell for their permission to use the letters of Dame Edith.

My thanks are due to the B.B.C. for quotations from 'Face to Face', 'This is Your Life' and 'The Brains Trust', and to the following newspapers: the *Sunday Times*, the *Daily Mail*, the *Daily Mirror*, the *Daily Sketch*, the *Evening Standard*, *The Times*, the *Times Literary Supplement* and *Time-Life*. Finally to G. Schirmer, Inc., for permission to quote a verse from *West Side Story* (Copyright © 1959, 1960 by Bernstein and Sondheim).

E. S.

CONTENTS

ILLUSTRATIONS

To Jeanne and Sherman Stonor

AUTHOR'S PREFACE

My years as secretary to Edith Sitwell represented a constant challenge, but no challenge was more formidable than the task of writing this memoir. To portray the many-sided, contradictory person she was and do justice to the fascination of her personality; to tell the true story of this, the Indian summer of her life, and to maintain the perspective demanded by the years that had preceded it—these factors alone would have made the book a difficult assignment. But there was an extra hazard. Because of Edith's tendency to confide in her friends about difficult situations or relationships and to leave her confidant with the impression that he or she was being uniquely vouchsafed the truth, any statement made about her is liable to contradiction.

It is necessary to make one thing clear. This is the Edith Sitwell that I knew. I have written this book because I believe that a study of the last years of her life can be of value and because I was privileged to be a part of those years. I have made it a personal account because only in this way can I be sure of presenting the truth as I saw it. But the portrait that emerges from these pages is a personal one. The stories that appear in them are the stories she told me, the echoes from her past are the memories that she passed on to me. Thanks to the great co-operation I received from her friends, I have been able to check the accuracy of what is stated here and, in so far as it is possible to do so, I have tried to be true to her personality in word as in fact.

To make the book readable I have refrained from peppering the text with sources. Her stories, opinion and comments are indicated by quotation marks. As she was the most articulate of women, her opinions have, in the main, been expressed in articles or lectures or comments to the press at some stage of her life. Her literary feuds, for which she was famous, have been lightly touched on, for the reason that, by the time I became her secretary, they had begun to subside. Her last campaigns, on the subject of animals and 'bad writers', are described in the final chapters, but must not be regarded as typical. The controversial Edith Sitwell will be recorded by people better equipped to do so than I, as will be Edith Sitwell the poet, lecturer, critic, journalist.

So, then, if the formidable Dame Edith appears in these pages as a human being with needs and weaknesses such as are possessed by us all, this is because mine is a study of the woman and not the personage. To put her in the perspective of her public image, I have quoted liberally from the newspaper reports over the years during which I was with her, but to understand strength one must first understand the frailties from which it emerges. Edith's courage triumphed over handicaps of which she herself made no secret. In understanding her handicaps I came to love her. It would give me the kind of satisfaction sought by all writers if, through reading this book, my readers feel the same.

PART I

The Beginning

Introduction

————◦⊖◦————

We all have the remote air of a legend. . . .
'Colonel Fantock'

ONE OF the penalties of becoming a legend in one's own
lifetime is that, in the end, the legend obscures the person.
By the time she was sixty-nine and I became her secretary,
the people who met Edith Sitwell for the first time were
meeting the legend. No matter how distinguished they were,
or how socially equipped, they tended to be self-conscious,
over-curious. They showed a desire to please rather than to
be pleased. And so did I. Less so, perhaps because I am an
Australian, and therefore was an outsider from the start; less
so, too, because there was a faint initial disapproval on my
part, stemming I have no doubt from nervousness and taking
the form of a general resistance to her bizarre appearance.

This was greatly enhanced by her dark glasses. I was to
discover how important it was to see her eyes, when making
the transition from legend to person, for their expression was
so kind, so lively, so much a reflection of the woman she was
that prejudice dissipated before them. The day I met her
was a day of high summer. The setting was the Aldeburgh
Festival of 1957, at which she read Blake in the parish church,
and she wore dark glasses throughout. The most formidable
of their kind, they had mirror rims that slanted diabolically
towards the temples. They were gold and black beneath a
Tudor hat that was studded with gold and framed by two
lengths of black chiffon. Her dress was of black satin and
worn to the ground; her Chinese coat was gold flecked by
green. Hands of great beauty, very long and delicately boned,
were weighted by aquamarines that flashed fire in the light
slanting through the stained glass windows. I sat in the back
pew with the friend who was to introduce me, filled with

foreboding. What kind of contact could there be between my prosaic self and so extraordinary a being? What communication would be possible between an expatriate detective novelist with one book to her credit and the *grande dame* of English literature, who looked like an incarnation of Elizabeth the First, who intoned Blake's mystical lines with the austerity of a Roman Catholic cardinal, who was, in fact, the embodiment of her legend?

How could one become secretary to a legend?

I should like to say that my forebodings were unjustified; that Dame Edith recognised my intrinsic worth behind the façade of indifference. In fact she did nothing of the kind. She took an instant dislike to me.

Not that I was allowed to see this at the time. Her manners were far too good. At the luncheon that followed the reading she was cordial if a trifle aloof. I drove back to London and wrote to thank her for the privilege of her invitation.

The result was a volte-face as typical as it was wholehearted. Edith Sitwell the woman had been touched by such appreciation from someone she had not only judged but condemned. She was remorseful. She answered my letter at once, asking me to become her secretary. When she returned to London she telephoned me.

'Well, my dear, may we take it as settled?'

No references were asked for; there were no tests to pass. I was summoned to drinks at the Sesame Club, her London residence. I walked through that uninspiring entrance with a sense of excitement sharpened by apprehension, conscious of a challenge that I was not at all sure I could meet.

I had been employed by the most controversial woman writer of our day, called a genius by some and an eccentric by most. I was to be at close quarters with a poet whose work I admired, to throw in my lot with a fighter facing the last campaigns in a lifetime of battle. I had been drawn into the aura of a living legend.

I would have eight years in which to get to know the warmhearted, insecure, intolerant, lovable person who had created it—Edith Sitwell the woman; the friend who signposted her friendship with an unvarying request:

'My dear, please do call me Edith.'

Chapter One

<hr />

I am as unpopular as an electric eel in a pool of flatfish.
Edith Sitwell to Robert Muller
(*Daily Mail*)

EDITH SITWELL was the most unpredictable of women. In her orbit contradictions manifested themselves as natural phenomena. The first of these, as far as I was concerned, was the Sesame Club.

Exactly why she had chosen this outpost of Victorian respectability as her London home remained as much of a mystery to me as it did to the countless friends who visited her there, until I became aware of her total disregard for her surroundings. The woman who had made an artistic tour-de-force out of her appearance never cared about, if indeed she ever looked at, a piece of furniture, the colour of a room, the pattern of a carpet. She ignored them with the sublime disregard of a being conscious that the world's attention was focussed on her and would remain, if not oblivious of, then at least prepared to disregard, her surroundings. Perhaps, too, the dramatic instinct that she possessed in full made her appreciate the value of contrast. By the time one had traversed the colourless foyer, the long corridor lined with chairs like the deck of a ship and occupied by old ladies who looked as if they had taken root and withered where they sat, and emerged, blinking, into the gloom of the little bar in which she entertained, the shock of coming into Edith's presence was great.

My summons was for drinks at five-thirty—'in order that we should become acquainted, my dear.' In such a setting she looked as exotic as an orchid in a field of turnips.

In the full glow of a July evening she wore a short fur coat over the brilliance of the jacket beneath. As before, the slender wrists and fingers seemed weighted down by jewels. A feathered hat defied the challenge of the fur. She was, one is tempted to say, enthroned in her seat beside the window, kept closed in all temperatures. Although it was a public bar, I found that her right of priority was undisputed and if some stranger had the lack of tact either to sit in her chair or to open the window, the heresy was never disregarded by the devoted staff. The trespasser was asked, politely, to move. The window was closed.

By then the pattern of Edith's life was established. Her summers were spent at Renishaw, the Derbyshire family home, her winters at Montegufoni, Sir Osbert's castle in the Tuscan hills. During the spring and the autumn, she was in London. She entertained. To the Sesame Club were bidden the literary élite, the titled, the famous; old friends, a manicurist down on her luck, a critic in favour, a foreign prince, a beat poet; anybody, in fact, whom she wanted to see at any given moment. Her luncheon parties could run to twenty guests at a time, her tea parties to a hundred. There were never less than four and there were always a couple of adoring young artists who were sufficiently 'sortable' —a favourite word of hers—to help her with her more difficult guests. They were invariably talented, invariably male.

I remember thinking, as I came into the room, that her parties must be the club's greatest attraction. There was an atmosphere of an audience about the people scattered around the room. From time to time gusts of whisperings were blown from group to group. I caught the word 'eccentric', and sometimes a hissing 'exhibitionist'. Their glances were as curious as good breeding would allow. They tried to catch her eye.

They did not succeed. Edith's attention was centred on her guests, as befitted a hostess with her exquisite manners.

'The trouble is,' she used to complain, 'I was brought up to be polite. It is the greatest possible disadvantage.'

On this first evening there were four of us: Alberto de Lacerda, the Portuguese poet; Gordon Watson, the pianist and my friend and compatriot; and, last but by no means least, Madame Evelyn Wiel, who, I learned later, had been 'left' to Edith by her sister Helen Rootham, Edith's governess and life-long companion. Madame Wiel was late in arriving and the three of us sat in a little circle around Edith listening to the beautiful voice that accorded each word the same light caress, whether it was to pronounce a blessing on a friend or to make mincemeat of an enemy.

The light played sideways across her face, revealing her principal claim to beauty, the smooth unblemished skin that was the result of a lifetime of protection from the sun.

Towards the three of us she radiated benevolence. We were her court and each one of us brought with us our gifts. The two men were established courtiers and brought the flattery of their devotion. I brought novelty. I was the new audience to listen and be charmed. The two men made a contrasting pair. Alberto de Lacerda was small, impeccably dressed, his dark eyes luminous with emotion, and poised like a dart-thrower to insert a compliment into the stream of conversation. His aim was unerring. He belonged to the history of such courts and his flattery was deft and informed. Gordon Watson played no such conscious role. Tall, with an exuberant vitality and a laugh that was loud enough to rattle the carefully socketed windows of Grosvenor Street, his appreciation was spontaneous if somewhat noisy. Both young men were widely read and both were genuine admirers of her poetry. Edith returned compliment for compliment, as lavish in her praise as she was content to receive it. Gordon was a 'magnificent' pianist, a 'genius'; Alberto a 'superb' translator, an 'excellent' poet. But it was not for nothing that her fingernails were painted the colour of blood. Her wit, I discovered, was very often spiced by a sense of the ridiculous that bordered on the malicious. An example of this was her comment on her old friend Madame Wiel:

'My dear, Evelyn is coming. She is nearly eighty and as deaf as a post but she has a passion for Gordon. We must leave the young people alone.'

I shall never forget the old lady's first appearance, nor the words that accompanied it.

Smartly dressed, her handsome, bulldog face distinguished by two fang-like teeth—all, alas, that had been left to her—

she entered accompanied by a volley of noise. Countless silver bangles, worn to the elbow, caused every movement to clash with the sound of cymbals. Her words, meant only for Edith, but audible, I'm sure, to the entire bar, emerged in a kind of booming croak, as deep, as melancholy and quite as penetrating as the frogs of Provence.

'Darling, I have come to meet the new secretary. Is that the one? But she is charming! Charming!'

Her inflection was one of surprise, as though answering doubts expressed in some previous conversation. Intensely embarrassed, I was grateful none the less, for by this time I was anxious to please. I had made a discovery. The formidable Dame Edith, before whom the valiant quaked, had turned out to be the most entertaining of women. I found myself laughing and knew that all was well. Contact had been established. Here was a woman who loved to amuse and I loved to laugh. The first hurdle had been jumped.

The main topic of conversation was the giant anthology she had been compiling, which, she said, 'really will be heaven. But just you wait until the reviewers find out that I have left out all the tiresome little Addisons and confectionery Elizabethans. What a loud howl will arise!' Only her discoveries among the early poems, she thought, would be exempt from their wrath.

In deference to me, she switched the discussion to the detective novel. To my relief it transpired that she—'like most poets, my dear. Dylan was mad about them'—was a reader of crime stories. In this, as in everything else, her taste was decided. Agatha Christie she enjoyed because 'she told an excellent tale'. Raymond Chandler was her favourite. Dorothy Sayers, although she conceded her one excellent book, *The Documents in the Case*, was definitely out.

'That awful Lord Peter Wimsey.' She put the tips of her fingers together to indicate all that she regarded as unsayable. 'Of course the trouble was, poor dear Dorothy knew the wrong dukes. I mean . . . they just aren't like that!'

As this was not a point that I could dispute, I contented myself by confessing with some timidity that I had enjoyed the Wimsey books.

'But then, my dear, you are an Australian,' she comforted me.

This was my first indication that the barrier of my nationality would prove to be a highly convenient one. It protected me from much, for the simple reason that I was not expected to know. I could confess ignorance with a free conscience. Any social blunders I might make could be put down to it.

There was a positive reason, too, why it helped. Edith was an aristocrat not only by birth but by upbringing. She had a mother who, as she says in her memoirs, in marrying a baronet had considered that she had married beneath her. '*I* am better born than *you*,' she hurled at her daughter in moments of rage. So it was not in the least remarkable that, although she had rebelled at an early age against the social conventions, Edith remained consciously the aristocrat in many of her attitudes, such as the intense pride she took in her lineage. But she was also the artist and so, paradoxically, had the artist's contempt for snobbery. She admired the new world and the robust individuality it produced, and she found it easier to establish natural relations with an Australian or an American for the reason that they were outside the hierarchy. With us she could be the artist, free of the prejudices from which the aristocrat could never escape. She could enjoy the vitality of Gordon Watson, and of Roy Campbell, the South African poet.

It was in a discussion with Alberto, who had known him well, that Campbell's name was brought up. She considered that he had performed a remarkable feat in digesting Baudelaire and re-creating his work so that his translations emerged as poems in themselves. 'But,' she said, 'Baudelaire lies in the French language more than any poet I know and should be read in the original.' No discussion, however, not even about poetry, remained on an abstract level with Edith, and she broke into anecdotes about him.

Her favourite story was one about the critic whom he had knocked down on her behalf:

'The critic never tired of insulting me and Roy decided to teach him a lesson. Roy was very big and enormously strong and he simply knocked him flat. The critic was terrified and crouched where he was on the floor. And Roy said,

"If you ever insult Doctor Sitwell (as I then was) again, you know what will be coming to you." And,' she added, 'he never did—until Roy died, and after that it started up again at once.'

Roy Campbell represented a great deal to her. Not only was he a poet whom she greatly admired, but he was that rare thing in her life, a champion. Perhaps because she had proved herself to be so formidable, it was not often that she was defended by her admirers and seldom, if ever, defended physically. She had an Elizabethan appreciation of a man who could use his hands as well as his head and she responded to Roy Campbell's championship with an entirely feminine gratitude. It was a source of sadness to her that she did not inspire a more protective streak in the men she liked. Whenever she was attacked—and, as she said herself, hot water was her native element—she would confide in me sadly, 'Nobody will defend me. You will see. Nobody ever does.'

From Roy Campbell to Dylan Thomas was a natural progression, but about Dylan himself she said little. I was to find out later that the mischief-makers had been at work. Someone had told her that Dylan had amused his pub audiences by giving imitations of her. This had hurt her deeply. Although she defended him as she defended Roy and was fiercely proud of her discovery of his work, there was a shadow over his memory. About Caitlin, his wife, she had no such reserves and made her the butt of her wit. However, Caitlin's book *Left Over Life to Kill* had been published shortly beforehand and Edith, to my astonishment, was kind about it. It had touched her sympathies, and also helped her to understand the woman whom Dylan, she told us, had so greatly loved.

'He would sit beside me, just looking at her. "Isn't she beautiful?" he would say. And I would answer, "Yes, my dear boy, she is." "You know, Edith, promiscuity is not important." "Of course not, my dear boy. Perish the thought!"'

'I like, "promiscuity is not important", don't you?' she appealed to us. 'Of course poor Caitlin was jealous of any other woman Dylan looked at.'

The conversation returned to poetry.

The reception of her *Collected Poems* had both delighted and depressed her. Cyril Connolly's 'Salute to a Major Poet' in the *Sunday Times* had made her very proud, but, she said:

'I've been beaten over the head by every poetaster and quarter-wit in England. One old girl compared me with Marie Corelli and I've had her pursued by human blood-hounds. It transpires that she is the mother—need I say?—of a clergyman of the Church of England! She had the impertinence to say that only my brothers admired my poetry. I wrote to her and said in that case Mr Yeats must have been my brother, which I never knew until now!'

For Yeats, she told us, she had a passion that dated back to her adolescence.

'I once left red roses on his doorstep. I ran away quickly before anyone opened the door but I think he knew who had left them. Of course he was an awful bore about women. I used to value what he said about my poetry until I read his letters to Dorothy Wellesley. She was quite a good minor poet but. . . .' The tips of her fingers came together.

She did, in fact, value what Yeats said of her work. In the months to come I came upon a record of a lecture Yeats had given as an old man in which he placed her in the top rank of the younger poets. She was delighted and insisted on the record being a feature of her tea parties from then on. I remember asking her, at this first meeting of ours, if she had known him personally.

'Goodness, yes. He used to visit me at Pembridge Mansions, and stay . . . and stay! One day he arrived at four o'clock and did not leave until seven. I lost stones. But I was flattered because he really is the most wonderful poet. Between ourselves, though, he was mean about money. I gave him the poems of mine that he put into his anthology and then he asked for "The King of China's Daughter" to be set to music and performed at the Abbey Theatre in Dublin for the sum of one pound. Of course I couldn't refuse, but. . . .'

Swinburne had also been an early love. According to her cousin by marriage, Constance Sitwell, Edith at the age of eighteen used to 'declaim' Swinburne to them. She told us now, the hooded eyes half closing in wry memory, how she had got into deep disgrace because she had been discovered reading him and how she had run away after his death and, taking a maid with her as a chaperone, had put flowers on his grave. Watching her as she talked, I marvelled at the delicacy of a body almost too frail to support its length and the contrasting toughness of a mind strong enough to declare its allegiance so early in life to a poet regarded as decadent by many of his contemporaries. I asked the inevitable question: who had been her first love in literature?

'Shakespeare,' she answered without hesitation. 'And of course Pope. I used to read *The Rape of the Lock* at night under the bedclothes by the light of a candle. It's a wonder I didn't set myself on fire. I had memorised it by the time I was twelve. It helped to pass the time, you see, on the long train trips to Montegufoni.'

Keats was another favourite. Wordsworth she was not so sure about, 'I always think I am not going to like him and when I read him I adore him.' Browning was a great poet, though 'he could be an awful bore at times'. About his wife she was devastating. The *Sonnets from the Portuguese* she dismissed as 'beautiful in emotion but. . . . They are simply not sonnets. The main trouble is, she is forever haunted by the shade of her horsehair sofa. She was the kindest and best of women but she had a rare talent for making great things small.' We might have remained where we were, entranced, for the rest of the evening, but for an incident that broke up the party. Two young men called to pay their respects. One of them was Malcolm Williamson, the composer, and, in common with many musicians, an ardent admirer of her poetry. Malcolm had invited her to attend a performance of a work of his and she had been unable to go. She had arrived back from the festival at Aldeburgh too worn out to be able to go out at night, but politeness now impelled her to exaggerate this and she told him that she had really been 'fearfully ill'.

Madame Wiel, listening to the best of her ability, heard the reason, if nothing else, and began to boom solicitude.

'Darling, you did not tell me you had been so ill. You must tell me when you are ill. You really must!'

'I *did* tell you, darling,' Edith said, with emphasis.

'No, darling, you did not. If you had told me I should have got the doctor at once. Perhaps you should see the doctor tonight.'

'Evelyn, I don't need the doctor!'

'But you just said you were fearfully ill. . . .'

There was only one way of stopping her. We got to our feet and made our farewells. My new employer extended me a hand.

'I shall see you tomorrow for luncheon, my dear.'

I don't know what I visualised in contemplating my new job. Certainly it was unlike anything I had imagined. It could not have been otherwise. I was to work for a woman whose life was her work, who could never comprehend that hours might be chopped out of a day and paid for. People were to say to me often in the years to come, 'She must be difficult to work for.' This was far from the case. That she was a perfectionist went without saying. She was a poet who declared that she had spent ten years in acquiring her technique. She was unlikely to tolerate a comma out of place on the part of a typist. Manuscripts must be accurate and they must be done at once. These were the rules, and once they were accepted, she was as appreciative as though the work had been done from kindness of heart.

What was difficult was that there were no precedents to follow. That first evening had given me an inkling of what was to come, but I would have been a great deal more apprehensive if I had known exactly where it was leading. Because of her age, because of her health, because of so many things, it soon became apparent that my duties were to be wider in scope than those of a secretary. 'I miss you as a friend as well as an aide-de-camp', she wrote shortly after she had left for Italy, and so it was to be. I was to help her entertain her guests, to become the recipient of her confidence, and the buffer between herself and the person who had provoked her wrath. I learned to protect her from the caprices she almost always regretted and, above all, I learned to reassure her.

It seems as remarkable to me now as it did then that this most famous and successful of women had no intrinsic confidence in herself. And yet it would be difficult to exaggerate the brilliance of her world. Not only was she acclaimed as a poet, but her way of dress, her outspoken attitudes, her literary battles, had established her as a personality everybody wanted to meet. Yet the woman who had projected her image with such success across the globe never quite managed to believe in it herself.

To portray this world as it was when I entered it, I will describe the first months of my new life, in Edith's seventieth year.

Chapter Two

———◦○◉○◦———

I am Virgo. I was born on the seventh day of September,
on the same day of the year and at the same hour as Queen Elizabeth the First.
Edith Sitwell to Elizabeth Salter

EDITH'S SEVENTIETH birthday, on September 7th 1957, was celebrated, if not with royal ceremony, then certainly with royal publicity.

I had arranged with her to finish the book I was writing before officially starting work, and so I was out of London at the time; but reading the newspapers, as well as the pile of cuttings she had kept over the years, I had a chance to take a leisurely look at Edith Sitwell as the world saw her.

The popular press was in love with her eccentricities, particularly those of dress. The *Evening Standard* photographed her in a Tudor-style hat and chose her as one of ten women they would put in the House of Lords, because 'some more magnificent background than lecture halls and poetry-reading platforms has got to be found for her, and as the Vatican or Chartres Cathedral are not available, the House of Lords is the only place left where she would look in her element.'

They were fascinated by the minutiae of her life: that she wrote in bed, for instance, 'so that her feet felt free' (true); and (untrue) that she 'slept in a turban'. The cuttings were filled with the more trenchant of her comments, such as: 'I am patient with stupidity but not with those who are proud of it'; 'People are usually made Dames for virtues which I do not possess'; 'I wouldn't dream of following a fashion . . . how could one be a different person every three months?'

The serious newspapers were concerned with Edith Sitwell

the poet. The *Sunday Times* printed a tape-recorded interview with her at which her old friend John Lehmann was in the chair and her 'supporters', as she described them—John Raymond the critic, William Plomer the poet and Sir Frederick Ashton the choreographer—asked the questions. They sketched her development from 1915, when she and her two brothers produced *Wheels*, their first anthology of poetry, and she was regarded as 'the terror of the Colonels, the horror of the golf clubs', to the present, in which she stood for them as the poet who had 'shown an unwavering belief in the importance of poetry and the status of the poet'. They discussed the influences that had helped to fashion her work: music, which played an all-important part in her youth, leading her towards her obsession with the sound of words, with phrasing and with rhythm; the country, from which, she said, came 'all the physical side' of her poetry, and where she had been 'much occupied in touching leaves and in seeing different aspects in things' and 'the relationship between things'; contemporary painters, such as Picasso and Tchelitchew; and poets.

Here, then, were two very different Edith Sitwells, both distinctly formidable and neither bearing much resemblance to the warm and witty hostess of a few weeks back. My fears returned, but were dispelled by the sound of her voice on the telephone.

From the beginning, she developed the habit of ringing me at nine-thirty each morning. It was an awe-inspiring experience, at first, to be informed in the impressive accents of 'Miss Mary', the club telephonist, that 'Dame Edith Sitwell wishes to speak with you.' But awe soon yielded to amusement. Inevitably she was upset about something and inevitably she was very funny about it.

Often it was a letter she had received that morning. Typical of these was one from a girl who had watched her on television: 'Just before going to work mum told me to turn on and look. I asked mum what you were like and mum said, "No chicken, and has to be seen to be believed".'

'For some reason the girl seems to think this would endear her mum to me,' Edith said. 'She sent me an enormous poem, commanding me to post it off to a paper, get it published and send her the money so that she could give her mum a spifflicating birthday present! Be an angel, my dear, and write to her for me. Tell her that I do not regard her mum's birthday as a cause for congratulations. Nor am I a post office. If I were I would charge for my services.'

Or it might be a press cutting in which she was misquoted —'Of course I never said anything of the kind'; or some newspaper had got hold of 'that awful photograph that makes a pet of all my wrinkles' or had gone on about her meeting with Marilyn Monroe. 'If I hear that dear girl's name again I shall shriek! Be an angel and ring the editor and tell him I scarcely knew her. Oh no, you'd better not do that. She might see it and then she'd be fearfully hurt. Do you think the little pets will ever give one any peace?'

This was not long after that much-publicised visit of Marilyn Monroe and her husband Arthur Miller to the Sesame Club. Edith had met the film actress while in Hollywood, where, in spite of 'working with great ferocity like a cannibal head-hunting', she had found time to talk with her and to listen to her stories of persecution from her fans. When Marilyn came over to make a film in England, she had arranged to bring Arthur Miller, whom Edith admired, to meet her. Arthur Miller was equally anxious to meet 'one of the most wonderful women I've met', as his wife described her. The meeting, reported as 'The Beauty and Brain Tea Party' or, alternatively, as 'Shape Meets Mind', was a personal success, spoilt, Edith said, by the reporters and photographers who filled the foyer at the Sesame Club.

'Uninvited, of course. So ill-mannered I think, don't you? I had to tell them to leave us alone. Of course they didn't and I gave them all a good slap to get on with.'

But the good slap did not prevent the press from exaggerating her acquaintance with Marilyn.

'One Egyptian paper said I was instructing her in philosophy. It really is too much.' In fact, she liked her and described her to me as a 'nice, quiet gel'.

'She simply listened while Arthur and I talked. She has a daffodil beauty, but in repose her face is strangely tragic. I said to Arthur that she should play Ophelia and he agreed.'

I was startled by this but could not help remembering it

years later, when Marilyn's tragic death was announced. Certainly it was the pathos of the world-famous star that had impressed Edith; shortly after their meeting, she wrote an article in which she described her as having the air of 'a little spring ghost', an oddly prophetic description of the 'unbreakable sex-fixation' of the cinema-going world.

Contrary to the popular conception of her, Edith had an aversion to publicity except for reviews of her books or her own public appearances. She would have been mortified if she had made a public gesture that went unremarked, but she regarded the private life of the artist as sacrosanct. 'Great men', she wrote in her review of Brinnin's *Dylan Thomas in America*, 'welcome that privacy to which the humblest of us is entitled and which should not, in my opinion, be denied the greatest.'

The intrusion of the press into her working life she regarded as persecution. 'Do you know, I used to write a little!' she would remark with bitterness, after a morning wasted in answering their calls.

One of my first assignments, then, was to deal with the press. This meant taking their enquiries and translating her replies. It was a never-ending process. When she was in London the calls averaged between one and three a day.

'Does Dame Edith approve of women in slacks?' 'Would Dame Edith care to comment on the tradition of four-poster beds?' 'What is Dame Edith's opinion of beat music?' 'I am doing an article on bed-warmers: does Dame Edith use the old-fashioned stone variety? Or does she wear a night-cap and socks?'

During those first months, before she left for Italy for the winter, and during her spring visit to London before going to Renishaw for the summer, my main occupation was to help entertain her guests. It is doubtful whether, at so early a stage, I was much help, but I was greatly entertained. Her diary was always full. Luncheon parties were followed by cocktail parties and there was an occasional guest for dinner. Her vitality was enormous.

In the midst of this frenzy of social activity Edith was proof-correcting the giant anthology that was being prepared for Little, Brown in America and was later to be published by Gollancz in England. To give some idea of the magnitude of this task, when the galleys were returned to her after publication they filled an entire post-bag. Edith, the perfectionist, was attempting the whole job herself, but her strength was giving out. 'My eyes are positively pairing,' she wrote to her friend Jeanne Stonor. Finally, she invited me and Alberto de Lacerda to luncheon and enlisted our help.

Proof-reading was no new occupation for me, but on this occasion I felt weighed down by responsibility. This was no ordinary job she had entrusted to us. Her anthology, and her *Collected Poems*, published earlier in the year, she regarded as the crowning of her life: the anthology was her treasure-house and the *Collected Poems* her life story.

It was not surprising, then, that two of the first among her guests that I met were the critics Cyril Connolly and K. W. Gransden, both of whom had given high praise to her *Collected Poems*. She made a practice, she told me, of thanking critics for intelligent appreciation of her work—a practice which may have been in part the cause of Dr Leavis's accusation that she 'belonged to the history of publicity'. In fact, if she did, it was for a different reason: she was as grateful for an appreciative review as she was angered by an unappreciative one. Whether this was due to the lack of confidence she was later to reveal to me, or simply because she set too high a value on the public assessment of her work, I could not decide.

Whichever it was, Cyril Connolly's statement that, when her poetry came to be compared with that of Yeats, Eliot and Auden, it would 'be found to have the purest poetic content of them all', ensured his welcome. Short and broad, with an impressive forehead above bland, oddly expressionless eyes, he arrived with his pretty young wife and some books for Edith to sign. I remember her answer to his question whether she had been conscious of being avantgarde when setting the literary fashion of the twenties.

'I never thought about it,' Edith said. 'I was just being myself. We were all of us just being ourselves.'

Gransden seemed to be as left-wing as Cyril Connolly was establishment. He had the slightly shabby look of the true

Hampstead intellectual, smoking, whenever he decently could, a Wilson-type pipe. I had the impression that he viewed Edith the woman somewhat less appreciatively than her poetry. Perhaps her anecdotal, sometimes scandalous conversation appeared frivolous to the man who had finished his review with the words: 'Edith Sitwell has something important to say. She may yet, in the years that remain to her, find a very great way of saying it. It is something to look forward to, such as we have not had in poetry since Yeats died.'

Celebrities now appeared on my new horizon in a crowd and names that had hitherto been associated only with my library shelves took on shape and substance.

The Stephen Spenders were old friends. Stephen, with his mane of white hair and strongly defined, sensitive features, looked to me a little larger than life. There was something idealised about his good looks, although his manner was unassuming and, towards Edith, faintly apologetic. Edith told me that she was never sure what *Encounter* was going to say next about her work. She was sincerely fond of him, however, and for Natasha, his wife, with her pianist's hands and her intense, Russian face, she had a sympathetic affection.

Sometimes her apparent affection for her women friends was not so genuine. I remember my first experience of what appeared to be downright hypocrisy on Edith's part. A friend had been invited to luncheon and before she arrived Edith grumbled about her as someone who was turning into 'a life work'. No sign of this, however, appeared in her greeting or in her manner during the meal. When her guest got up to go Edith invited her to come again, but expressed the profound hope, after she had gone, that she would not do so.

'Women are hell!' she said. She added, as an afterthought, 'Except for you, my dear.'

If it was hypocrisy it was not of the ordinary variety. I soon realised that Edith was the victim of her own politeness and was terrified of the demands that she might have led the other person to make, quite innocently, on her time. She was also capable of a dual emotion that pulled her in two directions at once. She could feel affection for someone and yet be irritated by them. Her irritation was partly nervous, partly liverish. I discovered that it did not do to take too much notice of the irritation. It was more likely to be the affection that was real.

Cecil Day Lewis and his wife, Benjamin Britten, Peter Pears and Sir William Walton were guests whom I met early in those first months. For Benjamin Britten she had whole-hearted admiration, and said of his setting of 'Still Falls the Rain' that it was so moving that she had 'relived the awful experience of having written it'. Cecil and his wife Jill, whom she described as 'a Greek beauty', were warm friends, but it was easier for Edith, I observed, to be enthusiastic about the work of an artist who was not in her field.

Her friendship with Sir William Walton is renowned. My own introduction to him coincided with the first of many discussions of the book which was to occupy Edith's attention, one way and another, over the seven years to come—*Lady Chatterley's Lover*. An approach from a film company, asking if they might use Renishaw as a background to their pro-jected film of the book, had been refused with indignation. Lawrence, she said, had used her family and her home as prototypes for *Lady Chatterley's Lover*. She appealed to Sir William to confirm this and, as I remember, he did so. Edith conceded Lawrence one good book, *The Plumed Serpent*, but apart from that there was no quarter given. He had trampled on her deepest loyalties and to the end of her life she denounced him. 'I am not and never will be interested in the goings-on to be witnessed on Monkey Hill.' Although she was in hospital during the 'Lady Chatterley' trial, she was furious that she had not been allowed to appear for the prosecution.

'A nasty, bad little book,' was her summing-up.

Edith's most frequent women guests at the time were her cousin Veronica Gilliat and Jeanne Stonor. Her friendship with Jeanne and Sherman Stonor had begun with a reading she gave at the Dorchester in 1957 in aid of the restoration of the beautiful little Stonor chapel, and remained firm in the years to come. Jeanne, small and dark and not unlike one of her own King Charles spaniels in appearance, was vivacious enough to be entertaining and staunch enough to provide a prop when Edith needed one. Veronica was her oldest friend, tied to her by the shared experience of fifty years or more. Her beauty was of the classical kind that does not diminish with the passing of time, and Edith admired this as she admired Veronica's dress sense, a quality in women of which she greatly approved.

'I could have been a dress designer,' she observed, 'and if I had I would have been a good one.'

This comment resulted from a press request that she be interviewed as one of the beauties of the day. She refused because, as she said to me, she was just an ugly old woman who had been clever.

Except for her hands, she insisted that she had no beauty. She disliked the word 'plain'; she thought of herself as ugly. The secret of her appearance, she explained, lay in the fact that she was as stylised as possible. 'I have my own particular elegance, but I am as stylised as the music of Debussy or Ravel.'

Choice of clothing, she said, was all-important. 'Very few women, my dear, are capable of resisting a fashionable idiocy. Suggest to them that they wear a dress for the simple reason that it is beautiful and, unless every other woman is wearing the same dress or something like it, they will refuse.' She was often quoted as saying that 'the trouble with most English women is that they will dress as though they have been a mouse in a previous incarnation'. To me she added that one must never try to soften one's worst features.

'I am tall and I have an acrid profile. So I draw attention both to my tallness and my acrid profile and make it look as though I were glad of them.'

Where men were concerned her attitude was quite the opposite. She considered it bad taste to notice how a man was dressed, unless he was too well dressed and then she was suspicious. One friend who could hardly be described as sartorially elegant was Jack Lindsay, the Australian-born writer, who, she told me, was 'a communist because he is a saint'. He owed his introduction to her to a review of 'The Shadow of Cain' which he wrote for *Our Time* in 1948. Coming to her notice during one of those fallow periods when everything she wrote was 'dragged out of the depths into the light and didn't like coming', his review revitalised her and helped bring her back to creative life.

'He was a really great critic,' she said. 'I felt as though he had lived through all the processes of my poetry. In those days I used to go nearly demented because of the lack of understanding of my work. Before the war nobody said anything about it, while the 1930 boys in their brown shirts with Liberty in large red letters all over them were scratching each other's backs.'

She never forgot the encouragement he had given her at that time and remained a loyal friend in spite of his politics, which she did not, of course, share. She had an added reason for being grateful to him, as it was Jack Lindsay who introduced her to the works of Lancelot Law Whyte.

I remember Whyte's arrival at her luncheon table because he startled me by throwing what looked like some children's blocks on to the table and asking her to select the design which attracted her the most. With an eagerness that was disarming in a man of science, he explained that they were examples of skew and symmetrical forms and were part of a study of asymmetry in which he was engaged. Edith made her choice and insisted that the blocks be passed round the table to the rest of us, delighted that her guests should become part of his researches.

The deference she showed towards the clever men of her acquaintance made her seem oddly youthful in their presence. Proof of this was Gordon Watson's reaction when I asked him, before I met her, how old she was. He was nonplussed.

'I have no idea,' he admitted. 'With Edith age doesn't enter into it.'

Towards Lancelot Whyte and towards Monsignor M. C. D'Arcy, who had instructed her in the Catholic faith, she showed the respect of a pupil. Their books were by her bed and she read everything they wrote.

Father D'Arcy and Father Caraman, her confessor, were regular visitors. Father D'Arcy was birdlike in appearance. Tallish and thin, with bright penetrating eyes under thick brows that dominated his face, his words accompanied by sudden movements of his tiny starfish hands, he looked weightless, as though nothing substantial held him to the ground. As a conversationalist he was the urbane man of the world, but his urbanity was combined with aesthetic fire and his brilliance with humility, so that for Edith he was friend as well as priest.

My introduction to one of the more celebrated members of the Sesame Club came one day when Alberto and I were lunching with Edith. Edith's position at the table commanded a view of the entire room and I heard her exclaim, 'Good gracious, here comes the Field-Marshal! With a stick, I see.'

I was seated on her right with my back to the entrance, and looked in a wall mirror to see who it was. Reflected from the waist up, I saw a broad, rather short, middle-aged man coming towards us, dressed in a jacket over bow-tie and shirt, with iron-grey hair waving crisply back from the forehead. I wondered which field-marshal it was who was beaming at Edith and approaching the table, and turned to face him only to discover that the Field-Marshal was wearing a skirt! It was Naomi Jacob. Bowing from the waist, she took Edith's hand and kissed it with masculine deference. I am almost certain I heard the click of her heels as she did so. In time I became accustomed to the sight of her when she was in London on her visits from Italy, leaping to her feet to stand to attention as Edith came into the room. On one occasion she asked Edith if she might present her with a relic 'as a token of admiration from one convert to another' and Edith, who was fond of her, accepted.

Her brothers, of course, were among the first visitors I met at the Club, Sacheverell before Sir Osbert, and I was impressed at once by the close family bond among them.

Towards Sacheverell Edith was the indulgent elder sister, devoted, convinced of his great talent, deeply, if sometimes irritably, fond. And, although her attitude in general to the wives of talented men was much the same as Gertrude Stein's, she made an exception in the case of her own family. Sacheverell's sons, his wife and his son's wife, were regarded as an extension of the two beings who remained the mainspring of her affection. She was aware of their faults, she would grumble about them, but they were, none the less, sacrosanct. If blame was to be attached to them, then someone else must be found to take it. She who had such a force of affection within her had made her two brothers, 'these two noble beings' as she describes them in her memoirs, the recipients of it. None of the stresses and strains that lay ahead ever seriously challenged her devotion.

Sacheverell was then in his late fifties, immensely tall, with thick grey hair, broad sloping shoulders, fresh complexion and blue eyes. In looks, at least, he seemed to me to be the typical Englishman. His mind was a storehouse of information and he kept up a rapid flow of conversation, as diverse as it was informative. One had the sensation, when talking to him, of being in a high wind, one's thoughts buffeted about by that searching, probing intellect. He asked a great many questions and sometimes, but not always, he would wait for the answers. Very often his question led him towards a subject that interested him and he would throw out information about it, not hopeful that the other person would contribute, but content to follow the darting firefly of his own interest. There was dissatisfaction in his expression but never in his conversation. Essentially kindly, his face creased upwards into an endearing triangle when he laughed, and it was at such moments that his likeness to Edith was marked.

'Sachie is the most talented of the three of us,' Edith remarked to me.

Towards Sir Osbert Edith's attitude was that of a younger rather than an older sister. Her respect for his character was boundless and her love for him had the quality of deference that I have remarked on before. He was the only human being about whom I never heard her utter a critical word. His illness was a tragedy to her. She suffered it with him, and her admiration for his fortitude was at once an anguish and a strength to her.

Five years younger than she was, he was then in his mid-sixties. His hair, like hers, had remained close to its natural colour and his fine head, with the 'Georgian eyes' as Edith described them, was leonine in its distinction. Because of his illness he spoke little, but his remarks were disconcertingly to the point and could be as trenchant as hers; his written words reveal the detachment that distinguishes him from his brother and sister and which has made him one of the great recorders of his time.

The admiration Edith felt for the talent of both her brothers has been jeered at as a kind of literary nepotism; but although publicly she was as generous in her praise of them as she was of any writer whose work she admired, privately she applied to their work the same critical objectivity that she applied to her own. She read and re-read their books, and if she did not approve of one she would say of it as she said of some of her own, 'It is not a good book, you know.'

Not all of Edith's guests were celebrated. Though conscious of the difference between the 'somebodies' and the 'nobodies', she accepted people for one reason only: she must like them. If she did, she would invite them to her parties no matter who they were.

This habit could be a source of annoyance to some of her friends, who might find themselves sitting next to 'that dear girl who used to manicure my hands' or a fellow club member who had provoked her sympathy. Sir Kenneth and Lady Clark, for instance, whose invitations were amongst the very few she accepted, seldom appeared at the club although they were valued friends. Sir William Walton was equally reluctant and quite blunt about it. 'I will come and see you any time,' he said, 'but not those awful friends that you surround yourself with.'

Their annoyance could be justified. I remember one 'club' friend who was to appear from time to time amongst her guests. She was a horror—a lady given to dirty fingernails and feathered hats, dressed with the aggressive bad taste of the well-bred Englishwoman. When I first met her she was making literary pronouncements on the subject of Charles Morgan. Edith had been asked to make a speech at his memorial service and was discussing the difficulties of paying a tribute that would be sincere without being a misrepresentation of her taste. I found myself listening to a dialogue that went something like this:

'The trouble is I really cannot say I like his books.'

'What nonsense, Edith! Of course you can.'

'I was very fond of Charles. He was a most courteous and charming man and he wrote one excellent review but. . . .'

'Edith, you are not trying to tell me he was not a good novelist?'

'No, my dear girl. I am saying that he was not for me.'

'Rubbish! I have heard you say the opposite.' To me: 'She doesn't mean a word of it, you know.'

After her departure I asked who the formidable lady might be, convinced that anyone who dared contradict Edith with such force must be a literary personage. I found that she was simply one of the many women who, over the years, had managed to pour out her troubles into Edith's sympathetic ear and so exercised a kind of moral blackmail over her. This one had 'come down in the world' and often complained to Edith about new club members who were 'not out of the top drawer', a phrase that amused Edith so greatly that she 'made a pet of it'. Towards Edith she adopted the proprietary air of a school prefect towards a lovable but erring member of her house. Edith, who appeared to be hypnotised by forceful women of this type, submitted to her bullying with a docility that would have astounded her literary opponents.

It astounded me, but then these were early days. I had much to learn—but I was learning.

Chapter Three

We are as cosy as a nest of tigers on the Ganges.
Edith Sitwell to a club bore

IN THE autumn of 1957 Edith set off for Italy. I rode in state
beside her in the chauffeur-driven Daimler to the station,
where, I discovered, she was as well known and very nearly
as ceremoniously treated as royalty. Only once did I ever
know her to travel by aeroplane and that was years later
when she was too ill to do anything else. For over fifty years
she had caught the train at Victoria and embarked on
the arduous two-day trip to Montegufoni. Nor was the
deference she received entirely due to her prestige. When
she asked me to distribute the tips with which she started
the journey, I had my first glimpse of a facet of her character
which was to represent one of the most serious problems of
her old age—her total disregard for money. The porters,
the conductor, her chauffeur, all received their 'presents',
and I am sure there are very few millionaires whose 'presents'
are more generous than hers were.

The train pulled out of the station and I was driven back
to my Hampstead flat. The first few months were over and
her letters from Italy began to arrive. Work by correspondence had begun.

My dear Miss Salter,
As I am feeling too hellishly ill to write . . . I am occu-
pying myself with arranging my new extended *Poet's
Notebook* which has to be done some time anyhow. So here
are the first few pages.
It has been a *mouvementé* morning. The Boy Friend [her

cat] keeps on walking up and down and then sitting on the
MSS and the priest has been ringing that damned bell of
his since 5 a.m. and all the Boy Friend's family and com-
panions are yelling in the garden!

My dear Miss Salter,
    Here is my new poem*. . . . Yes, my dear, I will be
grateful if you will send me one copy of the chapters of
The Queens and keep the rest.

My dear Miss Salter,
    Will you be so kind as to have the writing paper printed.
I think the address should be given as 'Renishaw Hall,
Renishaw, near Sheffield'.

My dear Miss Salter,
Please will you be very kind and answer this letter saying
that I have had to make it an invariable rule *never* to read
unpublished MSS.

On the back of each envelope was written:
Dame Edith Sitwell, D.B.E., D. Litt., D. Litt., D. Litt.,
    D. Litt.,
Castello di Montegufoni, Montagnana, Val di Pesa,
Prov. Firenze, Italy.

Manuscripts accompanied the letters once or even twice
a week, sometimes of a new poem, more often of a chapter
for *The Queens and the Hive*, and sometimes an addition
for the new *Poet's Notebook*, never completed, but which she
worked on as a therapy when overtired or bored.
    From her descriptions, and the occasional postcard she
sent me, I was able to add to the details of her background
already provided by Sir Osbert in his autobiography. I
could picture the twelfth-century castle with its tower, built
by the royal dukes of Athens, looking towards the rounded
Tuscan hills, the flagged stone courtyards, the fourteenth-
century lions mounting guard over the terrace lined with
lemon trees in huge terracotta pots and planted with zinnias
'some as high as my waist, some breast high', and with lilac,
mimosa and purple iris. Her room was in a wing of five rooms
leading from a passage 'frescoed by Severini and looking out

* 'The War Orphans'

over the Cardinal's garden'. In it and the room next door she worked, wrote her letters and read the books which flowed from one room to the other, growing upwards in stalagmite accumulations from the floor. When she worked she could stand no intrusion from the outside world—hence her complaint about the chapel, very beautiful, but so near that the bell 'was practically fastened to my bedroom window'. Fresh air was as much of an intrusion as noise, and any hint of a draught was attended to by Luigi, the energetic young butler, who stuffed each chink in her windows with tolerant thoroughness and saw that her shutters were closed for her regular afternoon sleep. Luigi, who was 'practically perfect', lived in the castle with his wife Elia and his three sons, and between them and their relations the work was done indoors and out. Being 'really frightfully intelligent', he not only superintended the making of wine and olive oil in the vast cellars behind the kitchens, but also acted as a member of the town council at Montespertoli, five kilometres away. In addition he waited at table (which meant carrying five courses up the flight of stairs leading from the kitchens), gave injections if required, and procured ping-pong balls for the benefit of Savonarola, Edith's beloved little clown of a cat.

Savonarola with the 'lovely sparkling white trousers and waistcoat, and the brown and yellow tail-coat' was a tremendous personality who liked nothing better than to 'frighten us out of our wits' by burrowing tunnels in the carpet, and 'biting my leg when I talk to people he doesn't know'. He was known as 'the Boy Friend' until the day of the 'appalling scandal', when it was discovered that Savonarola was a girl. 'Not only that,' Edith wrote to me, 'she has killed and eaten nine kittens! *So naughty!* She has now been accused of transvestism, incest, child-murder and cannibalism. But I won't hear a word against her.'

Her first letters were mainly concerned with post to answer, books to get for her or other people, papers to order, but they were always punctuated by comments to be savoured and enjoyed. She wrote as she thought and through her letters I began to know her. Although she was the untidiest of women, and mislaid almost everything that was sent to her, she was meticulous in her instructions and wrote plainly with very few corrections. Her kindness manifested itself at once, as illustrated by a letter which I reproduce in full. It followed an order for sherry to be sent to me from her wine merchants, as I was laid low with influenza.

My dear Miss Salter,

Thank you very much for your letter. I was particularly glad to get it, as I really have been *so worried* about you.

The sherry should have reached you already. If it hasn't, by the time you get this, will you please ring up Messrs. Matta and ask them if they got my letter and ask them to send you the sherry at once. I am nearly being driven *mad* by my book, I've gone dead on it. I can't tell you how much I look forward to *your* new book. Do send me a proof copy when you have one to spare, my dear.

I've had a very cock-a-hoop letter from a lady whose address I enclose. (*Need* I say that her Christian—well, perhaps not *Christian*—name is Desirée?) I do not know Desirée. But she writes to say that she has written a book on Blake, is 'looking for someone to write a preface' and that she had been told I 'would be ideal.'

I don't think she ought to spoil me, do you?

She also says she doesn't know if 'Blake is one of the figures who attracts me' (I having written about him at considerable length).

Will you please be an angel and write to her, acknowledging the receipt of her letter and saying that I only write prefaces under the rarest possible circumstances, and that I regret I cannot find time to do as she asks.

Or is that *too* rude? Should one say pressure of work prevents me? But I think she needs a thundering snub, don't you?

My dear, please will you be very kind and have two copies of this month's *Encounter* sent me, under separate cover (I mean the number that comes out this month) as I think Alberto's review of my poems is coming out in this number.

I send the enclosed chapter, not to worry you to type it

when you are ill but simply because I have nowhere here to put it.

Take care of yourself,
Yours most affectionately,
Edith Sitwell.

Good news followed. 'I've just been invited to be a Vice-President of the Royal Society of Literature, in company with Sir Winston Churchill and Willie Maugham, replacing dear old Mr de la Mare, Gilbert Murray and Max Beerbohm. This is fun, as I am the only woman, and it will be a crushing blow to my enemies.'

Her return to London in the spring of 1958 was earlier than usual in order to receive the William Foyle Poetry Prize, awarded after the publication of her *Collected Poems*. A little less nervous but not yet confident, I obeyed a summons to the Sesame Club, relieved to find one of her countless parties in progress. Either because of her terror of being bored, or because of her sensitivity to signs of nervousness on the part of a guest, Edith avoided inviting her friends to see her alone. During this spring visit of hers to London I was grateful for this. To me she was still a celebrity and it was only after our trip to Oxford in May, which I shall describe in the next chapter, that I began to feel at ease with her.

In the meantime a spate of television appearances led up to her June departure for Renishaw, culminating in a programme in which she was questioned by a group of schoolboys. This provoked the first of her letters from Derbyshire which ended with the exasperated comment:

'I had a terrible time—most fatiguing—talking to those stupefyingly boring little quarter-wits. The two boys would have *liked* to have been exceedingly impertinent—if they had dared. They didn't quite dare, but were on the verge all the time. They all had faces like badly made jam pancakes. It is monstrous to expect any serious artist to go and talk to such creatures, and very wrong to swell up their heads like this. Goodness!'

This letter had an added significance as it began 'Dear Elizabeth' and was signed 'Edith', thereby marking a step forward in my relationship with her. It also contained the postscript: 'My old enemy Mr Kenneth Young of the *Daily Telegraph* says it is now accepted that a certain famous line by Nashe *should* be, " Brightness falls from the hair!"'

But the Furies were manifesting themselves. There had been warnings earlier in that year of her declining health.

'I am in a good deal of pain,' she wrote later. 'I have either got intercostal rheumatism or have wrenched a muscle in coughing, which I do all the time. It is agony.' A few weeks later she had fallen and sprained her hand so that she could hardly write. And finally, as a result of hard work and constant interruptions, she reported: 'I have had only one hour's sleep last night and was violently ill, from fatigue and from having to work *and* have visitors.'

There were signs of increasing irritability. I had my first 'bomb' to send for her, in answer to a lady who had presumed on very slight acquaintance to send a manuscript for her to read. She had added insult to injury by addressing her as 'Miss Sitwell', which resulted in a reprimand that read like a roll of drums:

Dear Madam,

I am asked by Dame Edith Sitwell to tell you she regrets she is unable to read unsolicited manuscripts. She has no time in which to do so.

She feels, also, that if you consider yourself at liberty to approach her, you might at least address her correctly. Her name, as everyone knows, has not been Miss Sitwell for ten years. She is a Dame Commander of the British Empire and must therefore be addressed as Dame Edith. Before she was created a Dame her name was Doctor Sitwell, as she is an Honorary D. Litt of Oxford, Durham, Leeds and Sheffield Universities.

Yours faithfully. . . .

About another correspondent, who had corrected a reference of hers, providing some of his own work as proof that he was right, she complained:

'Did you ever see anything to exceed the blasted impertinence of the enclosed? Will you be so kind as to return the

whole boiling to the man and tell him that it is good of him
to teach me to write but unnecessary and, if he feels he
must bore me, I shall be obliged if he would address me
properly.'

And finally, having been 'pestered almost to death', she
sent me a batch of letters, all claiming her attention, with
instructions to send out 'the Form', a document concocted
by Sir Osbert and herself for the disposal of the most persistent of their 'pests'. Although I do not remember actually
sending it (in fact, my first act of flagrant disobedience was
not carrying out her orders to do so on another occasion), I
reproduce it here:

A. Name in full (block letters as throughout).
B. Specimen of usual signature.
C. Passport number. This must be accompanied by six
   photographs 2½ inches by 4 and these must be signed
   both by a clergyman and by a Justice of the Peace.
   They must also have been taken within the last six
   months. Old photographs cannot be accepted.
D. Finger-print number (if any).
E. When were you born?
F. Where were you born?
G. How were you born?
H. If not, why not?
I. For what purpose are you going there?
J. And if so, where?
K. Of what sex are you?
L. Age, sex and weight of your wife.
M. Father's name in full.
N. Mother's name in full.
O. Has any relative of yours ever been confined in a mental
   home?
P. If not, why not?
Q. If so, give full details with accompanying photograph.
R. Did you ever meet Burgess and Maclean, or anyone
   who ever knew them? This last must be accompanied
   by an attestation taken in the presence of a Commis-
   sioner of Oaths.

Fatigue did nothing to diminish the love of battle in this
rebel, who was as notorious for the demolishing of her critics

as she was for her loyalty to her friends. Her victim this time was the poet and critic Alvarez and her weapon was her review of his *The Shaping Spirit* which she had written for the *Sunday Times*. Accompanying the review came this letter to me:

'When I read the enclosed in which I have "taken care of" Mr Alvarez, who was impertinent to me in the *Observer*, my spirit is purged by pity and by terror.

I hope he will enjoy reading it as much as I enjoyed writing it!'

This was followed, on June 30th, by a cry of triumph:

'Yesterday I felt like a cat that had swallowed the canary, having read the *Sunday Times*, which really did me proud—what with Mr Maurice Wiggin's eulogy on my fearful adventure with those dreadful little quarter-wits on Wednesday and the printing of my relegation of Mr Alvarez to his proper place. The other day, I was told a story of a gentleman who met a lion in the desert. As there was no way of avoiding the lion, the gentleman knelt down and prayed. Opening his eyes presently, he saw that the lion seemed to be praying too. "How wonderful," said the gentleman, "to see a savage animal praying!" "Shut your trap!" said the lion. "I'm saying grace!" I hope Mr A. realises that *I* am only saying grace too!'

She was then working on her poem 'At the Cross Roads', and her letter dated July 1st contained an exciting promise:

'If I bring off the one I am working at, I shall dedicate it to you.'

But she was not at first pleased with it. In her letter of the following day she wrote:

'Your poem is all wrong. I shall re-write the whole thing. Don't be disappointed. I am going straight back to it now and it has the makings of something really worth while. You'll see. I'll send it probably in a couple of days or so.'

And so, on July 15th, the poem arrived, together with another, 'The Outcasts', which had been inspired by the refusal of the authorities to take any notice of the Wolfenden Report.

At this time I was writing a musical comedy with Malcolm Williamson. News of it leaked to the press, and to my annoyance, the paper made full use of Edith's name.

I wrote at once to apologise for it. Her answer came by return:

'What nonsense! Who on earth could possibly mind unless they were insane? I have just got your letter . . . and have already written to the Editor saying I looked forward greatly to your musical and that you are a very talented young writer.'

She went on to say that she had written to Hatchard's to ask for my books and had received a letter from them in answer, the content of which she repeated in full, knowing how much it would encourage me. I mention it as my first experience of the kindness that made anyone who worked for Edith devoted to her. Overworked and overtired as she was, she managed to find time to write three letters on behalf of her secretary.

Next day came an addition to the Everyman anthology, *Modern Poetry*, which she was compiling, with this comment:

'I think Lowell's "The Ghost" is, perhaps, the only *really* great poem produced by anybody younger than Dylan. It seems to me really tremendous.'

She had also made a new discovery:

'I have found a really brilliant writer—not exactly a detective story writer but a writer about crime. He calls himself Henry Cecil but that is not his real name. He is— as the librarian at Harrod's tells me—one of Her Majesty's Judges! Apart from anything else, he is really wonderfully funny!'

A writer who amused her being a pearl without price, she followed this with a request for more of his books, with the typical addition: 'And get copies for yourself, my dear, as a present from me.'

On August 18th came Sacheverell Sitwell's poems for the anthology ('Don't you think they're exquisite?') and a hurt little story about a young poet whom she had gone out of her way to encourage by inviting him to her parties, reviewing his books and introducing him to people he wanted to meet. He had written to her, 'asking me if I could get him a grant of money from one of the societies to which I belong to enable him to continue at the School of Dramatic Art without working in the evenings and at weekends (which would prevent him from writing). I wrote the day I received his letter to Denys Kilham Roberts, who wrote back to say he had told the young man in question that it was all fixed. Since then not one word!'

Compensation, however, offered itself. *The Threshold* by Michael Stapleton, another young writer whom she had befriended, had received acclamations from the press. She wrote so say how delighted she was about this and also described a letter she had received from Sir Maurice Bowra. 'He has been made President of the English Association and his presidential lecture is going to be about Yeats and myself—our poetry I mean (which will be a good slap in the face for Robert 1066 and all that Conquest etc.).'

'An American lady was found having a bath at Wadham College. The porter was deeply shocked and threw her out. Maurice does not know in what state of disarray!'

A new discovery was the work of 'that charming young man Mr Bernstein', who had been at Renishaw and had sent records of his musical comedy *West Side Story*.

'We have just got records of a very good musical from America,' she wrote. 'It is about juvenile delinquents and gang-warfare; and there is a heavenly court scene in which the young murderers, who have evidently been sent to a psychiatrist and caught his jargon, explain to the Judge that their behaviour is everybody else's fault, *not* theirs.

> 'My father is a bastard,
> My mother an S.O.B.
> My grandpa's always plastered,
> My grandma pushes tea.
> My sister wears a moustache,
> My brother wears a dress.
> Oh goodness gracious! Can you
> Wonder I'm a mess?'

She added a postscript: 'The *Times of India* says I have nothing to say and can't write and am neurotic. The *Times Educational Supplement* says my "vocal pyrotechnics" in the records were dazzling!'

The last of the material for the Everyman anthology reached me from Renishaw and by September she was ready to make her autumn descent on London. Her letters had given me an insight into the character of this creature of contradictions and conversations with her during the year had provided a glimpse of the influences that had formed it. To relate these conversations I must go back to the first trip I took with her to Oxford, where she recited *Façade* to a student audience, and when she talked to me, for the first time, about her life.

Chapter Four

I think that only
Winged ones know the highest eyrie is so lonely.
'Colonel Fantock'

FOR EDITH, the trip to Oxford represented a great personal success. For me it was in the nature of a revelation. It was the beginning of her acceptance of me as a friend and confidante, and over dinner on the night we arrived she began to tell me about the things that had happened to her: the funny things and the bitter things; the things that had moulded her, scarred her and inspired her; the things that had made up her life—although, she insisted, 'I have had no life'.

The menu did not please her, and she told me about her ancestor King Henry II, who had had 'all the chefs decapitated from London to Dover'. The wine pleased her even less. At her club she always ordered an expensive white burgundy, but for some reason on this occasion we had chosen a Graves. Edith took one sip and sent the bottle away.

'Wood alcohol!' was her verdict. 'Do you think we are poisoned, my dear?'

I had begun to realise that what she drank was more important to her than what she ate. It was part of her escape from the Furies which made her nights a torment of *angoisse* and which mocked her fame so that she could preface what she had to tell me with the comment:

'I cannot believe that I am anybody special. I am a maiden aunt, that is all. Just like any other ordinary woman.'

Sitting opposite her, aware that every pair of eyes in the room was focussed on her, I could not help reflecting that nobody looked less like anybody's maiden aunt. Yet she added, with bitterness, 'I am the changeling of my family. I do not belong and never have.'

In those words I glimpsed the sadness of her life. The story of her childhood she has told herself in her memoirs, and certainly it was the 'old unhappy far-off things' that came back to haunt her at the end of her life.

It was our mutual loathing of bluebottles, of all unlikely things, that sparked off her reminiscences. Blowflies, as they are called in Australia, are the bane of a hot climate and they remain the only creatures that I can kill without compunction. It was not so for Edith. Her horror of them dated from the time when her father had her put into the 'bastille', which she describes in her memoirs.

'I was thin and my body stooped slightly in a deprecating and rather frightened way,' she said. Accordingly a hideous contraption was designed to correct the curvature of her spine and—worst horror of all—her elegant and crooked nose, and into this 'bastille' she was locked every night. When she was thirteen and sleeping in the 'immense mullioned bedroom' at Wood End, there was a plague of bluebottles.

'In the interval of time between when my governess locked up my feet and when she came up to bed, I was alone, excepting for these fat, dirty, helpless creatures which buzzed about me, sometimes touching my face. When I exhibited my terror, a match-box was put in my hand, my wrist firmly held, and I was made to kill the bluebottles. "When this is over," they said to me, "you will be a different child."'

The result of this 'therapy' was that bluebottles became part of a hideous nightmare which she never forgot.

Judging from her own description of herself as 'possessed of the untidy elegance of a tall thin bird, wild and secretive with poetry, with an intolerance of stupidity and a passion for music', it is not altogether surprising that Edith's parents, who, she said, would have preferred her to have 'a profile like a Pekinese dog and a taste for lawn tennis', failed to appreciate her; nor were they alone in their disapproval.

At the sensitive age of seventeen, when dining with her grandmother, Lady Londesborough, she had been put next to a titled man with a taste for hunting who complained to her grandmother that 'she had insisted on talking to him about Brahms'. She was sent home in disgrace. Worse was to come. On her twenty-first birthday her parents arranged a house-party, supposedly in her honour. It coincided with the St Leger, and the entire party, consisting almost entirely of her parents' friends, was taken to the meeting. Edith's comment was to sit with her back to the races throughout.

This occasion, described so vividly in her brother's auto-biography, had burnt itself into her memory. Nearly six feet tall and inclined, even then, to rebel against the clothing bought for her by her mother, she presented a problem that her parents were incapable of solving. Although she remained openly critical of them and never yielded to a sentimental impulse to whitewash their memory, when she talked to me about them that night she was not as vindictive as she appeared to be later on, when suffering had accentuated the bitterness of her memories.

She told me that she was physically and mentally like her mother's side of the family, although 'they were practically centaurs and I could never get on a horse without trembling'. Her description of her mother I have never forgotten. She was very beautiful, she said, with a face that in youth had 'the pomp and magnificence of a Roman mask'. In old age the mask was 'still magnificent and its pride was unbowed, but it was empty'. Her neck and shoulders were statuesque, but, as if she were a statue, she moved with difficulty. 'Little things, water-drops or bee-wings, fretted her away and made her utterly unhappy. Much of her talk was full of these painful little cold water-drops, but there were moments when it flashed with brilliance.' She loved nothing better than to entertain, but her dislikes were as violent as her likes, and when she disliked she could be formidable.

'At one moment,' Edith told me, 'a lady who had not succeeded in gaining the approbation of my mother reproached her for never inviting her to the perpetual luncheon parties at Montegufoni. "Oh, Miss X.," my mother replied, "you always want to make the thirteenth at a party!"'

Her father she described as having 'much of the physical splendour of a fourteenth-century Italian noble. His dignity of bearing, his red beard, his rather strange pale eyes, all added to that effect.' And she went on to quote from her written description of him: 'He was born out of his century. His life ranged from the date eleven hundred to the end of the life of Queen Anne, and therefore he was never inwardly dull, as there were several centuries in which he could browse. But he suffered from the disabilities of the period, being obliged to watch bear-baiting, serfdom, tortures, etc. When he lived in that double life-time, he had much of the character of a bird on a bough, with a bird's strange detachment. He did not like modernity because it disrupted that inner spiritual life—it jerked his neck, like that of somebody being hanged. I think it was for that reason that he spent so much of his time lying down.'

A source of deep bitterness to Edith was her governess, Helen Rootham. This woman, who had been her companion for over twenty years and who had been the means of freeing her from her background, represented, from the viewpoint of her seventieth year, a prison into which she had voluntarily walked and from which she did not escape until her governess's death after a long and cruel illness. 'Complete freedom has only come in the last few years,' she wrote to Jack Lindsay in 1947.

Her attitude seemed a denial of the loyalty of which I knew her to be so abundantly capable and only after years of knowing her did it become explicable. Edith was all woman, but she was an unusual one, and in the days when the only escape from an unhappy environment lay in marriage, no man came along to offer it—at least, no man whom she found acceptable. Helen Rootham, a former governess and so a respectable chaperone, represented a way out to an independent life, and Edith responded with all the warmth of her nature to the gift of freedom that Helen brought. Two of the most important of her works, *Aspects of Modern Poetry* and her poem 'Gold Coast Customs', are dedicated to Helen Rootham; in a letter to Allanah Harper, who in 1929 was editor of the review *Echanges*, she asked that 'Helen might see Tom Driberg's poem, because she translates marvellously from French into English . . . and might be able to translate it into French'; in her own writings she quoted again and

[51]

again from Helen's translation of Rimbaud and never failed to give full credit to the translator. What she had not bargained for was the effect of her growing fame on her companion. As Edith became successful Helen Rootham became competitive, and her resentment showed itself in an attitude of increasing severity. A passionate woman, Helen fell in love with a 'bad painter' and spent on him all the money Edith had given her. Edith had been left the sum of three thousand pounds and had at once written out a cheque for £1,000 to Helen, together with £100 for her sister Evelyn. Unfortunately news of this reached her Aunt Florence, whose reaction was to cut Edith out of her will. This was a cruel blow to Edith who, although a daughter of a rich family, had, by virtue of her sex, very little in the way of a private income, and it added to the bitterness that was beginning to accumulate between her and her companion.

Helen managed the finances and saw to the housekeeping and the books she kept show that she carried out these functions with punctilious correctness. 'But,' Edith said sadly, 'as time went on she became more and more the governess and less and less of a friend.' She continued to treat Edith as a pupil, scolding her for her untidiness and reserving the right of restraint, so that, when she was over forty years old, Edith was writing to her cousin Veronica:

'I think I shall go to Venice for a week and stay in a quiet hotel and go sight-seeing with the Boyar*—as he screams at me to do by every post and sometimes by airmail. I shall have to pretend to Helen that I'm staying with people, as she'd kick up the hell of a row otherwise. She can't realise I am over forty, (alas).

'Tell me honestly, do you think I *dare* (being as aged as I am) stay for three or four days in Milan, on the way home, at one hotel with the Boyar staying at another hotel and go sightseeing with him? Or do you think my "good name" would be gone for evermore? I don't see why I shouldn't—do you?'

Helen's later illness, too, was a drain on Edith's vitality which the artist in her could not help but resent, the more so

---

* Pavel Tchelitchew, the painter.

because of the extent of her sympathy. She wrote to the same cousin:

'Helen—poor soul—has just been taken off to a nursing home to be operated on again for the same dreadful illness. When she came home (and they do not keep them for long in hospital here) I did all the nursing (she was entirely help-less)—and all the housework. And it was in the middle of the heat wave, which was worse here than in England. I was up at 6.30 every day and went to bed at eleven and was "at it" without stopping.'

There was little escape for Edith during Helen's illness. In 1937 she managed a visit to Spain at an hotel where the garden was 'a cross between a Douanier Rousseau and *l'Oiseau de Feu*', with 'enormous palms like fountains and a central pond . . . a pomegranate tree covered with dark coral flowers bending over it and reflected in the water . . . and nightingales (at the moment one is sitting on a bough of a lime within a foot of my bedroom window, yelling)'. But even then, worn out, no doubt by unaccustomed nursing, she went down with influenza, so bad that she thought her mind was going 'to swing about in empty space' for the rest of her life.

The end of a protracted illness can be very dreadful, and the nightmare of Helen's death in 1938 was enhanced by Edith's inherited horror of other people's illnesses; it is no wonder that, by the time she returned to Renishaw a few months later, her nervous system was so shattered, as she told me that evening in Oxford, that she was scarcely able to speak to the guests at her brother Osbert's table. 'I would just sit there, too frightened to say a word.'

There was another price to pay for Helen's illness, one that the artist in her resented with a passion that went deeper than her feelings as a friend. It is implied in this paragraph from Sir Osbert's *Laughter in the Next Room*:

'Alas, after 1929 began the long and mortal illness of our old friend Helen Rootham, and in the next decade, until Helen's death in 1938, the concern my sister felt for her, and the necessity she found herself under to earn money, com-pelled her to turn away from the natural expression of her being, towards prose; for some ten years she was obliged to abandon poetry.'

[53]

This alone was reason for bitterness, for at no time in her life did Edith enjoy writing prose, with the possible exception of *I Live Under a Black Sun*. But, as always, that evening she remembered an amusing incident *à propos*. It happened when she was still in her twenties and her ambition to become a concert pianist had not yet been finally banished.

Helen Rootham was not only a fine pianist herself, she was also a singer. She was asked from time to time to perform for her friends—'who,' Edith said, 'became grander and grander'—and one day an invitation came to sing at a soirée in a country house. Edith went along to accompany her and was introduced as 'Miss Sitwell, who is to play for me'. The butler, obviously primed for this contingency, swept the star of the proceedings off to the drawing-room, while 'Miss Sitwell' was asked to accompany him to a small room reserved for staff. Here her tea was served in solitary splendour, and she emerged only when called upon to take her place at the piano. After the performance was over, however, she had her revenge when her hostess began to boast to the company about an invitation that she was hoping to receive from Lady Londesborough to a charity ball.

'I shall see that my aunt invites you,' Edith said graciously, as she left.

From her stories, and the way that she told them, I was left in no doubt that the bitterness of the past overshadowed the success of the present. For the first time that night I saw her as an essentially unhappy woman, with too much spirit and too strong a sense of fun to be a defeated one, but conscious, in her old age, of the battle that her life had been and the scars it had left. And yet, as I write the words 'old age' they are as unreal to me now as when she uttered them. At seventy, before ill-health had seriously threatened her vitality, her age was the most unimportant factor of her personality. Her voice, the gestures of her hands, the quickness of her mind, defied the sum of her years. She had a child-like ability to submerge herself in her emotions and things mattered to her then as much as they had mattered when she was a child.

Not all her memories were unhappy. I asked her about the early days at Pembridge Mansions in which Helen and she had shared a flat for so long, and she told me about the people who came to her Saturday afternoon tea parties—Mrs Patrick Campbell, for instance.

'I liked her very much,' Edith said. 'Although, when I met her first, I hit her. I was in my perambulator at the time and she called me "baby". As I was four years old, I resented this.'

Mrs Campbell had been a friend of her mother's, and when she met Edith again after a passage of time her greeting was disconcerting: 'You'll never be the beauty your mother was, but you look at one so nicely that it doesn't matter.'

She was still beautiful then, Edith said. Unfortunately she never went anywhere without an embarrassingly uninhibited little Pekinese dog. Delighted as she was to see Mrs Campbell, Edith was not so delighted to see the dog, which was invariably asked to perform its tricks. 'After Mrs Campbell had got over her reluctance to enter the room,' Edith said, 'she would stand at the door shrinking back and exclaiming, "People . . . people . . . Oh, I can't face them." "No, Mrs Campbell," I would answer firmly, "you are well known never to have faced an audience."'

Mrs Campbell had made a 'great fuss' about the absence of tea-spoons. 'When she asked me why she had not been given one I told her that I was too poor to afford to buy silver spoons. Later on, after a success in a play, she sent me one dozen silver spoons. Between ourselves I was furious, but I knew she meant to be kind and so I kept them.'

Poverty had been a reality then. The flat on the fifth floor of a block without a lift had been small and simply furnished. Later on when I was furnishing her London flat, I collected what remained of her furniture. Most of it was the cheapest of its kind: two upright and rather rickety little desks of stained deal, an iron bedstead painted white, a folding table of the kind that graces most of the bed-sitters in London, one ample and comfortable chair, inexpensively upholstered.

They had lived with great simplicity, Edith informed me. During the war their diet consisted of 'nourishing' soup made by Helen and bread and cheese—although I suspect that time had encouraged Edith's imagination on that score.

During those early war years she even took a job at the Pensions Office until her health prevented her from going on with it. Looking at the exotic creature sitting opposite me, it was difficult to conceive of her as a young woman riding in a bus to work each day, even as a gesture towards the war effort; anyone further removed from the practical details of filing, typing or the management of money, it would be hard to find. Certainly this unlikely occupation left no mark on her personality.

In time, their life at Pembridge Mansions developed into a routine that suited them both. It was established that both she and Helen would work in the mornings; indeed Edith would often wake early and begin work at five or six o'clock so that she was finished by mid-morning. They had been able to afford a char, who was 'small and plump and objected to hard work but was willing to oblige'. They kept her on mainly because she was such excellent entertainment as she had the caustic wit of the cockney and a passion for funerals. 'It's your last chance, Miss, and 'alf the time it's bin' your first one, so why act begrudgin'?' Finally they employed a daily 'treasure' and trained her to deal with the 'pests' who increased in number as Edith's fame grew.

One of the first steps towards that fame had been the publication of her poem 'Drowned Suns' by the *Daily Mirror*. The great day was March 13th, 1913, when she was twenty-six years old. 'Tell Me Where is Sorrow Laid' followed in June of the same year, and then in September two poems, 'Love in Autumn' and 'In Remembrance'. In all, during the years 1913 to 1915, the *Daily Mirror* published eleven of her poems, and for this she felt a gratitude to that paper that she never lost. The enlightened editor of that time was Richard Jennings. Jennings became a personal friend and was invited in due course to 'sticky buns and strong tea', which was the fare offered at the Saturday afternoon tea parties. On the occasion of his visit, Edith told me, 'Tom [Eliot], Siegfried [Sassoon] and I read poems that we had discovered and everybody else had to guess who had written them.'

In 1915 her first slim volume appeared, *The Mother and Other Poems*—'sold at the time for sixpence, and now worth twenty pounds'—followed by the first issue of the anthology *Wheels* and *Twentieth Century Harlequinade*. By 1920 *Clowns' Houses* and *The Wooden Pegasus* had come out as well as *Children's Tales from the Russian Ballet* with a long and beautiful introduction that not only contained some of her best prose but showed how greatly the Diaghilev company had impressed her, even though, when speaking about it, she always denied that it had had any lasting influence on her. But this might well have been because she later changed her attitude towards ballet as an art.

'To tell you the truth, my dear, ballet bores the pants off me,' she remarked, at the same time admitting that Diaghilev himself had been a 'man of great force', and that 'no serious artist of his day could have failed to be influenced in some degree by his work.'

I remember thinking at the time that her withdrawal from so many of the interests of her youth represented not so much a change of taste as a decrease in her vitality, which instinct taught her to conserve for her first and real love, poetry. As she was not given to self-analysis—'I never think about myself except in grief and pain' was a much-quoted statement— she did not bother to ask herself why these interests had gone. She was content to dismiss them as 'a bore' and leave it at that.

In spite of having been described by 'that old bore, Angela Forbes' as 'plain and unsociable—I ask you, where has sociability led some people and where has unsociability led others?', Edith had always prided herself on being a hostess and, as her fame grew, the world climbed the five flights of stairs at Pembridge Mansions and was glad to do so.

Her stories of the now legendary tea parties were fragmentary. In the main they concerned distinguished friends who had begun their careers at this time, very often with her help.

She has written about Aldous Huxley at length in her memoirs as an early contributor to *Wheels* who remained a good friend. To me she described her last meeting with him in Hollywood, when he had taken her to visit Dr Hubble, an astronomer.

Dr Hubble, she said, was a man 'as good as he was great'.

He had shown them slides depicting solar systems in the heavens invisible to the human eye. '"How terrifying", I said, and he replied, "Only at first, when you are not used to them. Afterwards they give you comfort. For then you know that there is nothing to worry about—nothing at all."' Edith never forgot this conversation and quoted it later in an article she wrote on genius.

It was with the Huxleys that she dined with their mutual friends, 'nice Janet Gaynor' and her husband—'two people who are kindness itself, but who insisted on showing us their recent film of Africa. The impression we got was that Africa was a *very* large continent. Now, we would be told, we shall see a crocodile getting a baby hippopotamus by the leg—there would be a blinding flash and Miss Gaynor's face would smile at us from the screen!'

Although she was critical of his later work, Edith's opinion of Aldous Huxley's talent remained high—higher than her opinion of Virginia Woolf, whom she knew slightly in the days when the 'Bloomsburys' were at the height of their fame and influence.

'The trouble was,' she said, 'the Bloomsbury group civilised all their instincts away. They no longer knew the difference between one emotion and another. They civilised their senses away, too. People who are purely intellectual are an awful pest to artists. Gertrude Stein told me that Picasso, when he was a boy, screamed with rage at the superiority of the French equivalent of the Bloomsburys. "Yes, yes," he said. "Your taste and intellect are so wonderful. But who does the work? Stupid tasteless people like me!"'

Edith's criticism was directed more against Desmond McCarthy than against Virginia Woolf herself. 'Dismal Desmond' earned her wrath because of his poetry criticisms in 'those well-meaning weekly essays'. She quoted from a lecture she had given twenty years prior to our conversation in which she had said: 'The trouble with Mr McCarthy is an extreme mental timidity coupled with a rashness that, on the field of battle, would assuredly have won him the Victoria Cross. . . . He has a singularly defective ear . . . he hears no difference between the high accomplishment and magnificent rhythm of the band of the Grenadier Guards and the well-meaning but rather individualistic and wandering efforts of the village Band of Hope.'

She liked some of Virginia Woolf's work and had been greatly shocked by the tragedy of her madness. Because of this she was tolerant, not only of her fame, which she considered exaggerated, but also of her attachment to Miss Vita Sackville-West, about whom she had written in 1930: 'Miss Sackville-West, but for a flaw in fate, would have been Nature's gentleman.'

For 'Tom' Eliot, a friend of long standing and one of the early visitors to Pembridge Mansions, Edith had the greatest respect. He was 'a shy creature, always very carefully dressed', who looked, she said, what he was—a bank clerk. But she had also described him, in the lecture from which I have quoted above, as 'one of the greatest poets of the last hundred and fifty years', who had 'flooded himself with the immediate age as with vast oceanic tides', and she considered 'The Waste Land' 'one of the greatest poems of our time'. The measure of her feelings was displayed in her constant references to him both in letters and in conversation. 'When Mr Eliot, my brothers and I began to publish our poems, certain newspapers turned from their healthy and to me extremely exciting interest in crime and focussed their attention on us,' she complained. And in a letter to me about a young poet who 'had no hands for poetry', she made the comment: 'I do hate romantic wanderers, who are too great spirits to be in the city. Tom Eliot was a bank clerk for ages and is still a publisher.'

But, alas, at the time of which I am writing she no longer saw him. Deeply sympathetic about the tragedy of his first marriage, she was outraged by reports of his desertion of John Hayward when he married again. 'The way he walked out on that poor crippled man,' she said to me, 'just leaving a note to say he would not be back, after sharing a flat with him for so long—it was too cruel. But,' she added, 'I mind not seeing Tom. I was very fond of him.'

I wondered what mischief-maker had been at work.

Sir William Walton was, naturally enough, a visitor to those tea parties at Pembridge Mansions when he was just down from Oxford and was staying with her brothers in their Chelsea house. She described him as a good-looking young man, slim but 'extremely muscular—a fact that was not always understood by unfortunates who aroused his wrath'.

Their bone structure was sufficiently alike for him to be taken, as he once was, for her brother. Certainly he shared her intolerance for bores, and this and a youthful shyness meant that for some time he composed in the stables behind the house. At last it was decided to move the piano upstairs. All the morning workmen in green aprons attempted the operation without success, but that afternoon, when the Sitwells returned home, the piano was installed. When asked how he had managed it, 'Willie' answered, 'Quite easy. I just used a piece of string.'

One scandalous story that she told me about him I remember because of the comment with which she ended it. Apparently a certain by no means youthful female friend was determined to capture the young Walton, and while staying at Renishaw went to Lady Ida and accused him not only of having forced his attentions on her, but of resultant consequences.

'If it had been true,' Edith said, 'she would have left Abraham's Sarah at the starting post.'

I asked her how *Façade* had come to be written. 'It was a kind of dare,' she said. 'Willie gave me certain rhythms and said, "There you are, Edith, see what you can do with that." So I went away and did it. I wanted to prove that I could.'

Of course it was not as easy as that. Later she explained in more detail about the 'virtuoso exercises in technique', her experiments 'in the effect on rhythm and on speed of the use of rhythms, assonances and dissonances, placed outwardly and inwardly in different places in the lines in most elaborate patterns'. This was at a time when 'we, the poets, who had just emerged from that first world war felt as if a physical world and its manifestations were a new reality. They must be examined as if we had suddenly burst into life, or had gained sight after being blinded from birth.'

Her romantic interest during these early days was the painter Guevara, whose portrait of her hangs in the Tate.

He was also an early contributor to *Wheels*, but at the time of our conversation in Oxford her memory of him had been eclipsed by her stronger and more abiding love for another painter, Pavel Tchelitchew.

Another early contributor to *Wheels*, Wyndham Lewis, painted a portrait of her which, as he himself put it, waited for fourteen years for the 'Fifty Shilling Tailor' to buy it and eventually found its way to the Tate.

Wyndham Lewis was a never-failing subject for attack by Edith; in his autobiography he describes himself as her 'favourite enemy'. In a letter written to me later, she gave her reasons for this, perhaps the hardest-fought of all her campaigns, heading the account with a sentence under-lined—'*Everything comes to those who wait!*'—she went on:

'When I sat, many years ago, to Mr Wyndham Lewis, he was, unfortunately, seized with a kind of *schwärmerei* for me. I did not respond. It did not get very far, but was a nuisance as he *would* follow me about, staring in a most trying manner and telling our acquaintances about the *schwärmerei*. So, eventually, I stopped sitting to him (the reason why the por-trait has no hands). He revenged himself, in *The Apes of God*, by insulting me most grossly, calling me "a womaniser" and saying I had change of life! (I was about thirty-two.)

'When the book appeared, Mr Yeats wrote and reproved him very sternly, saying he understood it was meant for me. "If so, you are bemused." (I quote from memory.) "I thought when I read *Gold Coast Customs* that something had returned to literature which has been absent for a generation, and is rare in the literature of all times—passion ennobled by intensity, by endurance, by wisdom. We had such a man once. He lies now in St Patrick's, under the greatest epitaph in history." (Swift, he meant.)

'Two days ago, I had a letter from an American professor of a university, saying that, in conjunction with Mrs Lewis, he is editing Lewis's letters. That O. and S. had not been able to furnish any, but that he understood I had corresponded with him. That it would be a great pity if we were not represented in the book, so would I let them have these.

'I replied that I had never corresponded with him, but that if the letter written by Mr Yeats to him after he had very grossly insulted me in print were included, I should regard myself as amply rewarded.'

Lewis himself, however, did not appear to lose respect for her because of her attacks. 'Edith does liven up the English scene considerably,' he writes in his autobiography; and later: 'I'd a damn sight rather have Edith than those cowards who skulk beneath a nom-de-plume and peashoot you from ambush.'

In time, it must be admitted, her persecution of him became a kind of game which she enjoyed for its own sake.

'Whenever I was cross,' she told me, 'I teased Wyndham Lewis. I don't know if you ever saw him, my dear? He was always dirty, he wore a black patch over one eye, and a cloak and hat. Well, Osbert found a photograph of two 1890 actors who looked like him and promptly had them reproduced as postcards. Every day that man got one of those postcards, bearing the same mad inscription: "So there *are* two of you, Lewis?" And when Osbert's secretary lost a gold tooth it was done up in a jeweller's case and sent to Lewis, with Sir Gerald du Maurier's card enclosed—Osbert happened to have one!'

The story that ended our conversation that night in Oxford was about the youthful Tom Driberg, whom she described as 'one of the few grateful people alive'.

She had met him first when she gave a lecture at Oxford while he was still a student, and when he came up to London to make his way as a writer he came to see her. She had been greatly impressed by an early poem of his and admired his courage in pursuing his chosen course.

'He was working,' she said, 'in a fearful place—a kind of home for prostitutes and sneak thieves—for almost nothing at all. Of course he practically starved to death.'

This was an exaggeration, as the 'fearful place' was, in fact, a restaurant and Tom, provided with food as well as bed, was given the munificent sum of five shillings a week. But its clientele was much as she described it, and when the Sitwells arranged for him to have an interview with the *Daily Express* he agreed gladly to undergo a trial period as a reporter. So good was he that the Sitwells were thanked for their introduction, and thus began a career which led to his present position as a Member of Parliament.

One very minor event that happened on that first night of our trip to Oxford I shall never forget. As we went upstairs to our respective bedrooms Edith took off her hat. It was the first time in all the weeks that I had known her that I had seen her without one, and I had an odd sense of significance, almost as though I were present at the unveiling of a monument. The strange broad low slope of her forehead emphasised the hooded eyes and made the curving bone structure beneath them at once more delicate and more esoteric. The description, attributed to Elizabeth Bowen, came into my mind: 'like a high altar on the move'.

I went to bed with much to think about. The legend was being translated into a very human woman who, after so many years of fame, was still reaching out for sympathy and for affection. I recalled two lines from 'Colonel Fantock':

> For all the battles that this warrior fought
> Were with cold poverty and helpless age.

I wondered if 'life seemed less a stranger' to her as she stood before the cheering young audience who, on the following night, packed the town hall to listen to her read *Façade*.

Chapter Five

I would rather have my little joke than freeze on a pedestal.
Edith Sitwell in the *Daily Mail*, 1927

'THE FIRST public performance of *Façade* in 1923 raised an uproar among such custodians of the purity of our language as writers of Revue, firemen on duty at the hall and passing postmen, who, on being lassoed and consulted by journalists, expressed the opinion that we were mad.'

Such was Edith's own description of the launching of a work, which, thirty-five years later, in 1958 received a standing ovation from an undergraduate audience at Oxford. The performance had a significance that neither of us realised. It was to be the last time that she would recite *Façade* herself. The wheel had gone full circle. Unlike many other innovators she had lived to see her work span the gap between avante-garde eccentricity and popular acceptance.

But . . . 'It has come too late,' she said to me sadly.

At the age of seventy Edith preferred to entertain than to be entertained. She regarded a platform as her natural background and occupied it with royal ease. 'I am entirely unselfconscious,' she said, 'and when I am reciting it's like a bird flying or a fish swimming.' She was far from being an exhibitionist, nor was she, in the true sense of the word, an actress. Apart from certain readings from Shakespeare, she made no attempt to assume different roles for the benefit of her public. On the contrary, it was because she had been consistently true to her image of herself over the years that she had been able to project it to such effect.

'I am a Philistine,' she wrote in 1927. 'I intend to remain old-fashioned and in possession of my face however much of a natural disadvantage it may seem. I will also retain my own voice, my own manner, my own thoughts and my own phrases.'

When as a girl of eighteen she had rebelled against the tweeds, the boat-shaped hats, the fluffy evening dresses trimmed with water-lilies of her mother's choosing and had bought herself her first long black velvet dress, it was not only for the 'shock effect' of the dress itself, but because, she explained, 'I knew I was right to look different from other girls because I was different.'

It was this awareness of herself as a unique personality—so oddly contradicted by the moments of self-doubt that I have described—that made her so much at home in the public eye. 'The aim of flattery', she once said, 'is to soothe and encourage us by asssuring us of the truth of an opinion we have already formed about ourselves.' Perhaps Edith needed the flattery of public acclaim because it helped to keep at bay the insecurity that continued to threaten that opinion. Whatever the reason, there is no doubt that she enjoyed an audience and was at ease in their presence, particularly when she had been asked to recite.

On the whole she had looked forward to her appearance at Oxford, although aware of the tax it would prove to her strength. She was entirely professional in her approach, rehearsing for hours, both in London and at Oxford on the afternoon of the performance, and she was as nervous beforehand as are most good performers.

'It was worse when I was a girl,' she told me. 'I was simply frozen with nerves and so shy that my parents, in one of those ceaseless rumpuses by which they hoped to gain and hold the devotion of their offspring, called in Mrs George Keppel to scold me. Instead of which she turned on them and gave them a warning: "George and Ida, always remember that you never know what a young girl may become!"'

As privileged members of her entourage, her adored and adoring chauffeur (possessed of the inappropriate name of Raper) and I had been invited to attend the afternoon rehearsal. Edith was seated at her table front right of the stage, and the ensemble and their conductor, Peter Stadlen, were arranged in a semi-circle facing her. The famous screen which was to shield Edith during the performance had been painted according to the Piper design and was being constructed on a wooden frame, built for the occasion. Work on this was proceeding quietly in the background when, to our horror, we saw it pitch forward. It happened too quickly for anyone to scream a warning. Fortunately it missed Edith by inches and was prevented from crashing on to the heads of the instrumentalists by Mrs Peter Stadlen, who had been overseeing proceedings and who, with great presence of mind, threw up her hands in a backward movement which broke the fall. She was forced to her knees 'like Christ bearing the Cross', as Edith put it, but remained unhurt.

On the way back to the hotel she told me that *Façade* had been written 'for fun'. The audience was meant to laugh, but with her and not at her, as they had tended to do at first. She and William Walton had taken endless trouble to match words and music, and the screen was there to prevent the personality of the reciter from intruding and distracting attention from the surrealist patterns of image and sound which danced out their rhythms, complete in themselves. She herself read *Façade* in a strangely haunting chant, full of 'her own complex little distortions, more flexible and subtle than the strict metre of the music', as Peter Stadlen described it. She agreed that it was necessary to understand as well as to hear the word pictures, and for this reason had insisted from the beginning that the full text be printed in the programme.

Her attitude to the work was possessive. In fact, there were only two other speakers of whom she approved, Constant Lambert and Peter Pears; if it was read for meaning rather than rhythm, she disapproved. She herself always asked for a separate conductor to be with her behind the screen as she distrusted her own ability to read a score, in spite of her early training as a musician.

The result of such perfectionism was not always appreciated. 'By sacrificing emotion to rhythm,' one critic had written earlier, 'she produces an effect somewhere between a Greek chorus and a reading of a tenancy agreement.' But

that night at Oxford, the audience succumbed to the fascination. They laughed. They were silent. They seemed to be
aware of the privilege of being there. Her performance
would have been impeccable had there not been the slight
slurring in articulation which was beginning to trouble her.
The cheering audience brought her back again and again,
and she had to plead 'old age' and 'need to eat' before they
would let her go.

Both before the performance and at the supper party
afterwards celebrated visitors poured into Edith's hotel to see
her.

Lord David Cecil I remember vividly. Thin and nervous,
he sat poised on the edge of his chair, twiddling his thumbs
with an astonishing dexterity and leaning towards Edith as
though eager to absorb every detail of her complex personality. His stammering speech suggested that his voice was a
rein rather than a vehicle for the thrust of his thought.

Colin Wilson came backstage to see her and Edith, who
thought him a talented writer, agreed to review his *Ritual in
the Dark* when it came out. The study of a psychopathic
murderer seems, at first sight, a strange choice for a poet.
But Edith was 'interested in murder—I want to know *why*
people do these things'. The book appealed to her partly
because of the character of Jack the Ripper, who, she said,
'held the highly convenient tenet that the more one sinned
the greater the chance of salvation', and because crime had
always been a source of fascination to her. 'I once went to
have a look at 10 Rillington Place after the Christie murder
case,' she told me. 'It was a horrible lonely house. I felt
plainly that it was haunted.'

Towards crime, as towards much else, Edith was not con-
ditioned by middle-class attitudes. The violence and drama
of it found a response in her nature from which she never
flinched, however much it agonised her. She brought her
intelligence to bear on it. 'I think criminality is a form of
colour blindness,' she once wrote. At one period in her life
she was almost involved in a murder case through her kindness to a young writer, deformed and bitter and so unable to
find work. Edith, her sympathies touched, did her best for
him and entertained him at her club in an effort to show

him that the world was not in league against him, but she was not successful in finding him work. A month later she opened her paper and found that he had been accused of murder.

'It was some awful woman that I knew, and I felt sorry for him,' she said. 'But the friend who introduced me to him happened to be a lawyer. He put his foot down and said I was to have nothing to do with the case.'

To the end of her life, even when reading had become difficult, Edith could always summon the strength for an interesting study in criminology. Cruelty disgusted her, murder interested her. It banished her old enemy boredom.

Two of the younger and more notorious of her visitors at Oxford were Corso and Ginsberg, the 'Beat' poets. Edith had read and liked Ginsberg's poem 'Howl' and invited them to luncheon with her at her club. As this encounter was written up in a leading American magazine with rather more colour than accuracy, it might be as well to set the record straight.

She had chosen the inner dining-room of the Sesame Club 'so that the old ducks would not have so much to quack about', but even so we had to file past the tables of diners in their best tweeds and town hats. The procession was headed by Edith, leaning on her ebony stick, her tall cone-shaped hat worn above the long satin dress and inevitable fur coat. She was escorted by Quentin Stevenson, the young poet who had introduced the Americans, and was followed by myself and Corso and Ginsberg in their roll-necked sweaters, jeans and sandals. Ginsberg, with the 'look of a starving wolf' as Edith described him, and Corso, blue-eyed and seraphic, the stamp of innocence surviving his history of poverty and notoriety, were contrasts in themselves.

With Ginsberg on her right and Corso on her left, Edith proceeded to charm them into enjoyment. According to the magazine the conversation was devoted to the use of marijuana cigarettes and the menu consisted of cress sandwiches and tea. In fact it was a meal that had been especially ordered, beginning with smoked salmon and lobster thermidor and ending with the club's speciality, an ice-cream 'bombe à l'Américain'.

Edith began the discussion by remarking that she considered much of the vitality of the poetry of the present day was coming from America. She praised José Garcia Villa mainly because of his love poems, and went on to describe how he had come to the boat to see her off when she left the country 'with tears rolling down his green face'—green, she explained, because of a combination of his natural Filippino colouring and his grief at her departure.

American people, Edith said, really appreciated poetry. She found them 'warm-hearted, chivalrous and with beautiful manners'. She agreed that E. E. Cummings was 'the real thing' and mentioned her meeting with Marianne Moore, 'a delightful woman with the nature of a bird, very shy but friendly'. Marianne Moore had been made ill by her inability to cope with the letters of appreciation which poured in. 'People are so mercilessly kind,' she said to Edith.

The subject of drug-taking arose from a discussion about Aldous Huxley's experiments with mescalin. All three young poets admitted to the general use of marijuana amongst their contemporaries and defended it on the grounds of 'heightened sensibility'. Edith's answer, in no sense a judgement, was simply that 'no poet should need a drug to produce extreme sensibility, which must be, if he is any good, a part of his equipment'.

At this point she was not, as reported, offered a marijuana cigarette which she refused on the grounds that marijuana brought her out in spots. It would have taken a great deal more courage than any of the three young men possessed to have offered Edith a 'reefer'. Characteristically, when she read this account to me later on, it was not the imputation that she smoked marijuana that upset her as much as the doubts cast on her complexion.

'I am hardly the spot queen,' she complained.

What was remarkable about the luncheon was Edith's attitude towards her guests. At no stage did she talk down to them, nor did she dogmatise. She entertained, she listened, she commented. Her comments were different from those she made to her contemporaries in only one respect: they were kinder.

I knew she had had her doubts about entertaining them

at her club. In matters of decorum she remained the product of her Victorian training and she was well aware of the affront their appearance would represent to her fellow members. But the woman who had entertained Dylan Thomas for so many years and maintained that he had never misbehaved in her presence, was unlikely to admit defeat before the dishevelled Ginsberg and Corso. She bridged the gap in years, in background, in attitude, and was pronounced by them 'one of the angels'.

True, they had youth on their side, but what was more important, they had talent. This was the requisite for her approval. It was the dividing line between dismissal and encouragement that was always shown in deed as well as words.

Another result of our Oxford trip, and one which I am unlikely to forget, was the outcome of a performance of Schoenberg's 'Pierrot Lunaire' by Hedli Anderson in the first half of the programme. It was the first time I had heard this twelve-tone work with its unpredictable intervals, its downward and upward swoops that reminded me, irresistibly and irreverently, of the back-yard cats of London howling to each other. When I got back I gave a demonstration to my friends which lost nothing by the early training I had received as a singer. It was meant to end there, but, unfortunately for me, my performance was reported to Edith, who not only insisted on hearing it, but enjoyed it so much that it became a party piece requested on all occasions, appropriate and inappropriate. In fact, on looking back over those seven years, I cannot remember an appropriate occasion. Confronted by the startled faces of her fellow club members interrupted in their peaceful mastication by my piercing yells, and by the baffled amazement of the eminent guest for whose benefit I had been asked to perform, I cursed my imitation and prayed for the day when it would be forgotten. It never was. Edith, who disliked the music, would laugh until the tears rolled down her cheeks. She enjoyed it so much that I never had the heart to refuse her, although there was one occasion when I came close to doing so.

Edith had rung me one morning and announced, quite

casually, that Sir Alec Guinness was coming to luncheon. Would I like to come and meet him? I accepted with gratitude, and looked forward to the meeting—that is, until I remembered 'Pierrot Lunaire'. She wouldn't, I thought. She couldn't. But she did. Ten minutes after being introduced I had to get to my feet and 'do my imitation'. I felt like 'the greatest fool of all time', in the words of Edith's telegram to Sir Alec after his own performance in *Lear*.

Sir Alec, another eminent Catholic convert, was an old friend. Her poem 'Invocation', written as far back as 1943 and included in her collection of that time *Green Song*, had been dedicated to him and his wife Merula. A quiet man of medium stature, his expression conveyed the melancholy introspection of the contemplative rather than of the actor. He was obviously eager to discuss their religion. In fact, his reason for coming to see her was to apologise for an account of her entry into the Church which had appeared in an American magazine and which had been credited to him— a highly coloured, irreverent description which owed more to imagination than to fact, and from which Sir Alec was anxious to dissociate himself. The Aquinas volumes she had given him, he told her, meant a great deal to him; so much, that he was unhappy unless he had them with him. I was not surprised to hear him say that his role of the cardinal in *The Prisoner* had been an unforgettable agony to him.

Listening to his talk, I was aware that here was an actor who would sink his own personality in a role rather than project his image through it or, as is so often the case, in spite of it. His comments about his profession were illuminating. From the beginning, he told us, he had watched people's feet: the way they walked told him much about them. His ability to imitate was so deeply ingrained that when, in his youth, he had received a letter in a markedly individual hand, he had found himself replying to it in the same handwriting.

The impression he left was of a man with a vocation and a genius within that vocation, but remaining, because of the depth of his nature, unsatisfied by it.

Chapter Six

My rule is to deal with everything that maddens me at once
and then turn to what interests me and even with luck do a little work.
Edith Sitwell to Lancelot Law Whyte

ON THE morning after luncheon with the 'Beat' poets, a
new precedent was established. Edith's nine-thirty telephone
calls became post-mortems on the events of the day before,
which usually began with the question, 'Was it all right do
you suppose?' On this particular morning she added, 'Do
you think we have been given fleas?'

A new threat to her health was revealed. The *angoisse* that
she so often suffered during the night had been so bad that
she had been forced to take some brandy in order to
sleep.

'I have inherited *angoisse*,' she told me. 'My father had it
so badly that he would walk up and down all night. I used
to hear him when I was a girl.'

There was the usual 'pest' letter. This time it was from
an Australian. 'I'm sorry to tell you, my dear, that she is a
compatriot of yours. She tells me that my name is really
Harris—which for some reason infuriates me. That she is
therefore a relation of mine and that her 'Harris Aunts'
have written to a Mr Somebody-or-other of whom I have
never heard and who will bring her here! She had *better*
come!'

I offered to deal with the Harris pest and she answered, as
always, 'Will you, my dear? That would be kind.'

A process was at work between us, never mentioned but
tacitly understood. Her irritation with her 'pests' served as
a therapeutic focus for the anxieties and frustrations of
growing ill-health and personal disappointments. She would

ring me in the first flush of anger and give me minute and terrible instructions as to what to say and how to say it, from which I would extract the essence and send off a mild letter designed to give offence to none. It had taken me some months to bring about this state of affairs, and had not been possible until I had been given permission to answer her correspondence personally. When really enraged, she would still write out a 'bomb' herself, as only by the writing of it could she exorcise her wrath; but as it was usually given to me to send, she knew and I knew that it was unlikely to be sent.

Not that I wish to soften her image by any sentimental interpretations of my own. In her last eight years she used her 'pests', worthy or unworthy, as targets for her wit. They were also a favourite complaint.

To Jack Lindsay she wrote, 'I have got several very bad new lunatics, including the daughter of a nursery maid who left us when I was eleven and whom I have never seen since, and the vision of whose daughter has been, by the grace of heaven, spared me. She absolutely pesters me. When my father died, she said she intended to come and live at Renishaw to help us. "I will bring my bike and run messages." Where to? To Heaven, presumably. I expect she would have brought her "mac" but she was warded off.'

Then there was the leper's stepmother.

Leprosy was, at this stage of her life, much on her mind. It had a special horror for her, containing the elements of terror and doom which tuberculosis must have had for Thomas Mann when he wrote *The Magic Mountain*. 'I am horrified to hear from Graham Greene that he is intending to stay for two months in various leper colonies in the Congo,' she wrote to her friend Jeanne Stonor. 'Adventurousness can go too far. But I am telling him he must regard us as moral lepers and come and see us first.'

He did not, however, manage his visit until his return when, delighted as she was to see him, both as a friend and as a writer for whom she had intense admiration, she was somewhat nervous about contact with him.

'I shall just have to say to Graham, "My dear boy, I could not be more pleased to see you, but if, by any chance, you should want to sneeze, then please go to the window and sneeze out of that.'''

She was convinced that the disease was passed on by sneezing and was by no means sure that Graham Greene had not contracted it. She also believed that it would not show itself for fifteen years. 'And we don't want that ahead of us, do we?'

A newspaper enquiry after her health happened at about this time, and with Graham Greene on her mind she answered that she had 'every disease known to man except leprosy'. This called forth an irate letter from the stepmother of an English leper, who told her, in round terms, that it was nothing to make light of. Edith, who was very far from making light of it, wrote an immediate letter of apology. Vastly encouraged, the lady began a 'Laocöon' correspondence which, according to Edith, meant at least one and sometimes two letters a day.

This assault on her time was tolerated partly out of horrified compassion and partly, it must be admitted, because of the revelations on the part of the afflicted lady, whose husband had attracted the attentions of the police through a compulsion to reveal more of himself than is legally considered suitable.

'The leper's stepmother is pursuing me at every turn,' she wrote to me. 'Her husband has undressed publicly again. He is seventy-eight and has taken a job as a night watchman. They have, in toto, £12.'

The lady was not slow in capitalising on what must have been to her a most gratifying response, and, although repeating that she did not want anything from Edith, she began making comparisons between herself writing her letters in poverty, clad in her husband's worn-out dressing-gown, and Edith receiving them in bejewelled splendour. In fact, except for the gloves which she invariably put on to open these letters for fear of infection, Edith was in her normal working attire, which consisted of a knitted bed-jacket of her own making and a long and practical night-gown. She was incapable of resisting moral blackmail of this kind and each time would order a hamper of food to be sent from Harrods to the value of five pounds. Having done this, she would take off her gloves, answer the letter herself and prepare to give her guest of the day a blow by blow account of the latest revelation.

This state of affairs continued, remarkably enough, for very nearly a year. Then, at last, her letters to me showed signs of increasing irritation. 'The leper's stepmother is driving me to dementia. . . .' 'The leper's father has been undressing again and the police have nabbed him. . . . I am getting a *bit bored*.' Finally she yielded to my persuasion and the correspondence ceased.

It is easy to be wise after the event. Looking back on the years 1958 and 1959, I can see now how much she allowed 'the clothes' moths to fritter away my brains', as she put it. Her waning vitality was being drained, not only by the kind of correspondence I have just described, but by challenges of work that she never failed to meet, by public appearances, by the endless parties she gave at the Sesame Club. Day after day I was called in for luncheon and for drinks at five-thirty, and asked to arrive early to discuss the seating at her table and to be 'briefed' about her guests.

I would find her waiting for me in her corner of the bar, looking as fresh as though she had just got out of bed (which, in fact, she had done, as she worked in bed) and smelling of the scent that she liked to blend herself. As might be expected, she had managed to manufacture an aroma uniquely hers, experimenting with various brands, so that her movements were accompanied by a fragrance never overpowering and never quite recognisable. Often she would be talking to Kate, the bar-woman, one of the devoted attendants in whom she showed an interest, or to the manager, Mr Murphy. Punctuality was the strictest of Edith's disciplines and I cannot remember an occasion when I was there before her. Usually she presented me with a tiny chart on which she had worked out the seating of her guests, but she was never content to leave it at that. One of the most disarming of her attributes, which endeared her to all who worked for her, was her habit of consulting one on matters of protocol. Nor was mine the only opinion that was asked. She was quite capable of discussing a social problem with Kate or Mr Murphy and of listening to the advice they gave her. The flattery of this is evident, but it was not calculated on her part. People to Edith were all individuals to be judged according to her caprices. Their significance in the world was kept in a separate bracket in her mind and had little to do with the small events of ordinary living.

If her parties were not always successful, it was through no lack of hospitality on her part. She planned the menus with the same care that she gave to the seating of her guests. They were usually lavish, with liberal quantities of wine. Her close men friends were called upon to act as host— Cecil Beaton, perhaps, or John Lehmann or Gordon Watson. It was a two-edged compliment since, far from being in the position of privilege on her right, the host usually found himself at the other end of the table, forced to be polite to the wife of some other eminent guest.

There were times when her memory failed her. I remember one occasion when a luncheon guest was announced who was waiting in the hall. Edith had omitted to make a note in her diary and the table was already full. I had to face the new arrival with the disconcerting tidings that there was no room for him, offering, as consolation prize, an invitation for the following week.

For some reason the television companies who pursued her with requests to appear often chose the lunch hour in which to contact her. Once, while she was entertaining two television personalities, Mervyn Levy and John Freeman, an invitation came from 'People and Places' to appear as a local celebrity in a programme to be shown in Yorkshire and Derbyshire.

'Tell them that I haven't the time, my dear,' Edith instructed me. She added, 'I wouldn't mind if it were England and Wales, but I absolutely refuse to be crowded into a couple of counties.'

I remember a Catholic party that she planned, because it was my introduction to Allanah Harper, former editor of *Echanges* in Paris and now Mrs Robert Statlender. Edith once described Allanah to Graham Greene as 'a convert whom the late Aga Khan wanted to marry, because he was so astonished that she returned the diamond bracelets which he hid under her napkin. As time went on, the bracelets increased in number, size and value, but she always handed them straight back with the terse enquiry, "What's that for?"'

Guest of honour at several parties was the writer 'Bryher'. Described in the papers at this time as a 'reluctant millionairess', she was a shy but generous patron of the arts and Edith was profoundly grateful to her for her practical encouragement over the years. Small and weatherbeaten, her appearance was dominated by eyes as blue and as tranquil as the fictional sailor's. Her dress was simple: she affected the dark suit, blouse and beret popular in Paris at the time of Sylvia Beach. The result was deceptive and was the cause of a favourite among Edith's stories about her.

A 'titled bore' of her acquaintance invited herself to a poetry-reading that Edith was giving in Bryher's honour, especially to 'meet the millionairess'. As she arrived late, she could not be introduced, although placed next to Bryher. During the first half of the programme her eyes wandered discontentedly through the ranks of the audience. Finally when the interval came she turned to Bryher and complained, 'I can't see the millionairess, can you?'

'No, I can't,' Bryher replied gravely.

Comparatively new friends were J. W. Lambert of the *Sunday Times* and his wife. I remember their first appearance because of a story Lambert told about the Greek actress Paxinou. Edith, who was seldom enthusiastic about any actress other than Edith Evans, told us that seeing *Electra* in New York had been one of the greatest experiences of her life.

'The rhythm of the mourning,' she said, 'like perfectly regular waves beating upon an immense shore, the ineffable style, majesty and elegance, moved me beyond words. And Paxinou herself, dumpy, arms too short—and what did it matter? One looked only at her and listened to that voice. She was superb.'

Lambert then said that he, too, was an admirer of Paxinou and went on to describe his first glimpse of her. It was during one dark and stormy night of the war, when, as a young seaman on a destroyer, he was sent to man the scrambling nets thrown over the side in order to pick up some survivors in a lifeboat.

'Suddenly, in the dim light,' he said, 'there emerged out of the sea that extraordinary profile surrounded by wet hair streaming in the wind. It was like a goddess figure from Greek mythology. I knew that this must be some out-of-the-ordinary person and as soon as I could I found out who she was. It was Paxinou.'

Crises were the order of the day. 'I do think life is *mouvementé*, don't you?' was a recurring complaint. But she needed her crises as she needed her pests. Very often the product of her own nervous irritability, they provided the opposition against which her productive energy flung itself and so flourished, though this forced growth took its toll.

'My American publisher has asked me to sign my name eight thousand times over for the anthology!'

'My dear, the temporary typist has made the most fearful muddle over the Swinburne MS. My entire reputation would have been ruined.'

'Elizabeth Jenkins' fine book on Elizabeth the First is just out, with a great deal of new material in it. The whole of *The Queens and the Hive* will have to be written again.'

'That old bore next door to me goes to the loo without stopping all through the night. So pleasant for the rest of us.'

American visitors represented recurring crises that began with the nine-thirty telephone call and ended in large luncheon parties, especially lavish as a return for the generous hospitality she had received in the States. Amongst them were the poets Isabella and Allan Tate, the writer Gore Vidal and 'Betsy' Whitney, wife of the American Ambassador in London at the time. Tall, elegant, with a soft voice almost devoid of accent, her manner towards Edith showed the affectionate deference that characterised so many of her American friends. In fact, looking back over these years, it is the warmth of her American visitors that separates them from the others. They held nothing back. The English, though proud of her, reserved the right of criticism. They admired her but did not 'go overboard' for her. To the Americans she was Queen Edith.

Hazel Guggenheim, the artist, illustrates this in her description of a party given in Edith's honour. When she was taken up to be introduced, she found Edith so hemmed in by admirers that she was scarcely visible. They sat on the floor, their adoring elbows pressing on the antique sofa on which Edith was enthroned. So much weight on such antique legs resulted in the collapse of the sofa, a contingency from which, she said, Edith extracted herself with dignity and the willing hands of her devotees. Edith's memories of her visits to the United States in the decade following the war remained amongst the most carefree of her life. It was for this reason that she welcomed the visits of Billy McCann to the Sesame Club.

Billy McCann was a friend who dated back to the Pembridge Mansion days, where, as a small boy, he lived in the flat below hers and was reproved for staring at the strange being who appeared on the stairs. During the war he became head of the Iberian section of the Ministry of Information and, Edith said, 'lived the life of one of Peter Cheyney's heroes'. His home was in New York and during the lecture tours and poetry-readings which took Edith up and down America, they met again. He was part of the reception committee that watched her arrival in a flying boat on the Hudson river, from which she was taken with due ceremony to the Astor estate for a weekend house-party. He was on the station in Florida when she arrived for a short visit, nearly fainting from the heat because of the fur coat she insisted on wearing, and accompanied by no less than twenty-two pieces of luggage, most of which were filled with books. He was a constant visitor to the St Regis hotel at the suite that was always made available to her and, most important of all, he was a friend of Pavel Tchelitchew, who was now living in New York.

Another bond between them was his love of wild creatures, and his appearances invariably resulted in a fund of anecdotes on the subject, two of which she related in a letter to Graham Greene:

'All my news consists of travellers' tales, the principal being the adventures of Billy McCann. . . . He has a *mania* for birds. On his way through New York to Janeiro he paid several visits to a pet shop and there a macaw was seized with such a romantic admiration for Billy that, every time he went into the shop, the bird would faint dead away and fall off its perch. So Billy thought it would be only kind to buy it. This he did, then realised he would never be allowed to take it on the plane. He had it drugged, therefore, and made it into a large paper parcel, which he nursed on his knee. Unhappily, the bird came to, half way through the flight, and the woman sitting next to him said, "Must your parcel wriggle and fidget and poke me in the eye?"

'Another time, during the worst heat wave they had in Rio for years, looking out of his window at the boiling ocean, he saw, to his amazement, what appeared to be an enormous company of people in evening dress—immense white women and very tiny men in dress suits proceeding across the ocean to the shore. This struck him as odd. As the procession drew nearer, he saw that it was a vast company of polar bears, penguins and sea elephants.

'Poor boys and girls, they had been sitting quarrelling on an iceberg at the South Pole, when the iceberg melted and they were precipitated into a current which bore them, willy-nilly, to Rio. Billy rang up the zoo, which sent down quantities of ambulances with ice, and the whole lot of them are now sitting happily on ice at the zoo. When captured, they were fainting from the heat.'

Her love of animals being one of the abiding passions of her life, stories of her own and other people's adventures with them were inclined to crop up at unexpected times. One of these is for ever associated in my mind with the arrival of Sylva Norman to a luncheon party at which Edith was to read her new poem, 'The War Orphans'.

Sylva Norman, Edith told me, was the former wife of Edmund Blunden and her champion during the *Spectator* controversy of 1954 when 'Anthony Hartley failed to recognise a quotation from Donne and abused it violently.

'I was in Hollywood at the time and cabled the editor suggesting that he have Mr Hartley stuffed and put in a glass case with moth-balls at my expense. This was because, at one stage, when the *Spectator* was being more than usually pompous, I sent the Editor a stuffed owl, suggesting that he should give it reviewing as, at any rate it had recently been combed for moth. I sent the cable out of sheer fun, but it did not exactly go with a swing. The *Spectator* was furious, especially as the *New Yorker* took it up and had a drawing of a reviewer in a glass case being shown to companies of school children.' Sylva Norman, writing under the pseudonym of Laura Deane, wrote the only letter that was printed in her defence. 'It was most awfully good,' Edith said. 'She told them that she would be sorry if I allowed myself to be pecked off Parnassus by the dicta of fledgling poetesses who aim to make their nest there and finished with the hope that I would continue to truss, poison, bastinado, roast or fry—in effigy of course—my adverse reviewers!'

As a result of this letter, Sylva Norman became a friend who was usually invited to gatherings such as this one. The other guests were also reviewers or poets, and after the meal we made a circle around Edith in one of the club drawing-rooms and waited for the reading. Edith picked up her manuscript, told us a little about the poem and then, for no apparent reason went off at a tangent with the words, 'When I was kissed by a lovely girl gorilla.'

Although not quite what had been anticipated, this was an opening to command attention. Edith went on to tell us how she had been taken to an American zoo and introduced to the 'lovely girl,' who was about to be mated but who had taken a violent dislike to her fiancé and was in a difficult mood. Edith was warned that it would be dangerous to show any fear, as wild animals interpret fear as a sign of hostility, but, as Wyndham Lewis once said, Edith was 'as brave as a lion', especially with regard to the animal kingdom, and she had no hesitation in entering the cage. 'Whereupon,' she said, 'my hand was seized and my glove pulled off. This long black paw with the removable skin was obviously a source of fascination and she tried the other one. Then she lifted my palm and smelt it for a long time. After that she threw her arms around me and kissed my cheek. I was never more flattered in my life.'

Usually, if she had a new poem to read, she made it an occasion for a tea party, an 'all-in massacre', as one of her friends put it, that sometimes ran to eighty guests. To these tea parties she invited those fellow members who had forced their way into her acquaintance by storming the citadel of her good manners. She avenged herself by giving each one an unflatteringly appropriate label. There was 'Snake Eyes', an immensely tall, sinewy woman whose eyes glittered in an alarmingly reptilian manner. The 'Blue Meringue' was a lady of rounded outlines who suffered from the conviction, shared, alas, by all too many, that Edith was devoted to her. Another was the 'Vampire Trout', who was a source of comment because she was very rich (which was not held against her), rather elderly (which was), and because she revealed a persistent and predatory interest in her brother Osbert. About the 'Vampire Trout' Edith told us that a portrait had been done of her by a woman who 'loved painting old ruins'. 'She has threatened to send us her head, which is rather like my darling little cat who was found the other day putting a dead mouse in my bag.'

At her club, if left alone for an instant, total strangers would converge on Edith and pour out their troubles into her unhappily sympathetic ear. Only if they said the wrong thing was she able to snub them, and then they would receive the pent-up resentment of other frustrating encounters. She would recount the stories of these snubs with relish, enjoying the picture of herself as a 'tigress' ready to devour.

Her favourite concerned the lady who squeezed herself into the lift with Edith and informed her that she was 'so sorry to have missed your little concert'. As this was a recital at the Royal Festival Hall that had been booked out months in advance, Edith was justifiably annoyed.

'We *all* missed *you*,' she said sweetly.

To the woman who came up to her, gushing that she had longed to meet her ever since she had read one of her brother's books, Edith replied, 'Then let us postpone the pleasure until you have read one of mine' and departed.

Unafraid of wild animals or public platforms, Edith had one fear to which she confessed freely: she was mortally afraid of bores.

'I am one of those unhappy persons who inspire bores to the highest flights of their art,' she said.

This was a family trait, resulting, no doubt, from inherited good manners. Her brother Sacheverell was once pinioned by a garrulous gentleman at his club. 'I do hope

I am not boring you,' his persecutor said at length. 'It doesn't matter,' came the suffering reply.

A bore for Edith could be anyone from a 'good conversationalist bent on wrapping up nothing whatsoever into something that will make you look silly', to the 'sweet, interfering, bat-witted old ladies' by whom she was surrounded. Her closest friends, if they made the mistake of recounting their experiences on return from abroad, could be bores. Politics bored her and also scientists who 'insisted on sending up mice to badger the moon.' She was never bored by a person who knew his subject and talked about that. She was never bored by scandal, by crime, by good poetry, or by wit. It is not surprising that the poet who spent a lifetime trying to 'see things as though seeing them for the first time' might be bored by the small talk of the average person, the colour of whose words 'came out in the wash years before'.

Repetitious Edith certainly became, but she was never a bore. The care and skill with which she chose her words gave her conversation a unique sparkle. She used to quote the answer given by her brother Osbert when asked how he could tell good poetry from bad. 'If it is good it is fresh, if it is bad, it is not. If in doubt try it on the cat.' Edith applied this test to her entire vocabulary, and as a result she was the most quoted woman of her day.

Chapter Seven

I have received as much adulation as a film star . . . except perhaps
for Miss What's-her-name, who looks as though she's been nibbled by mice.
(*Daily Mail*)
Edith Sitwell to Robert Muller

TRAVELLING WITH Edith was always an event. It happened rarely, even in those early years, but there were occasions when 'the Motor' was summoned and we would sally
forth, well wrapped up by the imperturbable Mr Raper in
a fur rug against the English summer. It might be for a drive
round the park in the spring to see the cherry trees in flower,
'looking like young girls', or to catch a train, as happened
when she went to Manchester for a television programme.
It was never simply a matter of going by car; it was always
referred to as 'the Motor', a suitable title for the big black
monster that would wait, purring, outside the club, with Mr
Raper at attention beside the door, one of the porters ready
to help Edith into the back seat and a little flurry of passers-
by stopping to stare. People in the street recognised that ours
was a motor with a *personnage* inside. Curious glances followed us. Our arrival anywhere was guaranteed to attract
a group of spectators to whom Edith, who accepted them as
her due, never failed to extend a hand. It was a royal gesture,
stemming partly from courtesy and partly from 'an addiction
to liking people of all kinds'. With Edith there was no automatic classification such as is practised by most of us. No
hall porter, no lift attendant, was passed without greeting.
The camera crew were accorded the same respect as the
producer of a television programme. Before the start of a
journey the train guard must be summoned in order to be
introduced.

This was no affectation on her part. Forty years of fame

had taught her to expect a reception from the curious where-ever she went, and her training from the early days of her childhood when she stayed with her grandmother, Lady Londesborough, had equipped her with something of the royal manner.

That formidable lady must indeed have been queen of her domain. When they travelled by coach, Edith told me, they were accompanied by four and sometimes six liveried attendants. On their return, a carpet was unrolled to the steps of the coach to protect their shoes from contact with the earth. Servants were never addressed personally by Lady Londesborough. Instructions were given through the butler or the housekeeper, the only two beings, apart from her personal maid, whom she considered worthy of direct communication.

From her second grandmother, Lady Sitwell, Edith learned a different facet of the aristocratic conception. Here was a Lady Bountiful who distributed her largesse amongst the under-privileged and occupied much of her time in good works. Edith, whose reaction against the poverty and affliction she saw around her as a child was a 'black shadow over the secret heaven' of her imaginative life, saw that compassion, to be effective, must result in action. It was a lesson she never forgot, although at times her actions reflected not only the influence, but also the economic values, of her grandmother. On the way to the Manchester train, she caught sight of a pitiable bundle of rags delving in a rubbish basket beside the road. In these days of National Assistance, we can comfort ourselves with the reflection that the person has brought it on himself. Edith, however, for whom the words National Assistance were meaningless, ordered the car to stop at once.

'Be an angel, my dear, and give this to that poor creature,' she requested.

It was a half-crown piece that she handed me. The look of startled wonderment on the face of the recipient remains with me to this day.

The royal manner she acquired, the Lady Bountiful she sometimes was, but the assumption of class superiority implied by both attitudes she rejected. Her recognition of the right of all human beings to be regarded as individuals was more than an intellectual concept. It was a reality that contradicted the public image she so fiercely projected, of the Plantagenet whose critics could not forgive her because she was a 'lady'. Her snobbery was reserved as a weapon against the snobbish; it had no bearing on her affections, which could be gained as readily by a housemaid as by a duchess. Wherever she went there was a devoted attendant in her orbit, whom she thought about and wrote to as a friend.

There was Velma Le Roy, for instance. Velma was her chambermaid at the Hollywood hotel in which she lived while working on the film script of *Fanfare for Elizabeth*. Edith became genuinely fond of this 'angel of a Negress' and never forgot her. When the B.B.C. chose Edith for its 200th edition of 'This is your life', it was because of Velma Le Roy that she consented to appear. Although this programme was supposed to surprise its subject, her health at the time was so precarious that, had she not been forewarned, she would not have been allowed to appear. She was, in fact, strongly advised against doing so, but when she heard that Velma had been contacted and offered a flight from America, she did not hesitate. 'I could not dream of disappointing her,' she said.

A retainer whose devotion was not quite such an unmixed blessing was Hannah, her former housemaid at the Sesame Club. Hannah was Welsh and given, Edith said, to nervous breakdowns. In spite of them, or perhaps because of them, Hannah remained a fixture in Edith's life. For any recital that Edith was to give, tickets must be sent to Hannah. Nor were they merely put into the post. They must be given to Mr Raper to deliver in person to the Carlton Club where Hannah now worked as a chambermaid. 'Because,' Edith explained, 'it makes her feel important and that cheers her up.' When Hannah retired, she was invited to pay a formal visit to Edith at least once a month. Her fares were paid and an envelope containing a pound note was given to her on departure. Birthdays were never forgotten and when, during one of Edith's spells in hospital, one was overlooked, Hannah rang me to remind me of the omission.

'My lady must be taken bad,' she repined. 'Not once in all these years has she forgotten me. Not once.'

Hannah was also the source of a story which Edith delighted to tell against herself. Hannah's early devotion had been given to her mother, a lady who, she informed Edith, had resembled her in more ways than one.

'Plain she was, my lady, but proud. She would sit outside her door on a Sunday morning and the preacher would go by after chapel and point her out to his congregation. "There sits a good woman," he would say. "Plain she is, God help her, but a lady, look you." And so are you, my lady, so are you.'

It did not surprise me, then, when at the start of our journey to Manchester Edith asked for the guard to be summoned in order that he might be introduced. I left him talking to her about the length of his service on that particular line and went to buy a crime book, a transaction which served the double purpose of giving Edith something to read on the train and filling her purse with silver for distribution en route. After a suitable length of time a 'present' was delivered into his hands and he went his way, promising her eternal devotion and privacy on the journey.

Her appearance on television was the result of a correspondence that had sprung up between herself and the painter Mervyn Levy after the publication of his book, *Painting For All*. Levy had met Edith when they had been fellow guests on a series of Sunday afternoon television programmes in the early 1950s. She was impressed by his book, which, she told him, was further proof that painters often make excellent writers because of their acute and vivid sensibility, whereas poets seldom make good painters. They had shared a friend in Dylan Thomas, and her decision to appear with him at Manchester was influenced by the fact that two portraits of Dylan Thomas were to be the chief subjects of discussion. One was by Levy himself and the other by John. Augustus John was an artist about whom she had reservations; she believed that he drew what he thought should be inherent in his subject rather than what was in fact there.

Edith herself had been approached by John on more than one occasion to sit for him, but the final arrangement which was made by George Rainbird, the publisher, in 1956 had been cancelled by John for reasons of health. In the letter of apology he wrote her, he stressed: 'I have long wanted to draw you and I do hope you'll give me another chance.' But the other chance never came, perhaps because of her misgivings about his work or perhaps because, after sitting for so many artists, she could not face the prospect of another. On the programme with Levy, she was openly critical of John's portrait of Dylan Thomas, so much at variance with her own description of the poet who, when she first saw him, looked 'like a youthful Silenus if Rubens had taken it into his head to paint him'.

A personal reason for remembering our trip to Manchester was my introduction to the work of James Purdy, Edith's most recent 'find'. She had given me his *63 Dream Palace* to read on the train, marking each story in her own order of preference; so, while she nodded gently over the latest Agatha Christie, I began on the grimly beautiful novella after which the book is named.

Her discovery of James Purdy, she told me, represented a minor mystery that was never solved. She had gone to sleep one afternoon at Montegufoni with windows shuttered and doors closed against draughts and intruders as was her custom, and when she woke up there was a book lying on her bed which had not been there when she went to sleep. It was called *Don't Call Me by my Right Name*. The first story she read concerned two Negro mothers in Chicago, and, convinced that she had stumbled on a great Negro writer, she read the remainder only to discover that the author was a white American of Scottish-Irish ancestry, living in New York. As always, when impressed by new talent, she wrote to the author, and through her recommendation *63 Dream Palace* was published in England by Victor Gollancz. The result was a new and lasting friendship with another young writer, who wrote to tell her that she had become his 'patron saint'.

Although in general reviews of *63 Dream Palace* were not quite what she had hoped for, her own review in the *Times Literary Supplement* brought this response from Purdy:

'I was quite annihilated by your wonderful review of my work . . . I feel like a man who has come out of Plato's cave and looked at the sun! I do want to be worthy of your tribute,

Dame Edith, and I will spend the rest of my life writing in the hope that I may.'

She continued to extol his praises wherever and whenever she could. 'A writer of genius,' she wrote to Pamela Hansford Johnson, 'who, long after my death, will be acclaimed as one of the greatest writers ever to come out of America.'

Whenever she was asked, as she often was, to recommend books that had impressed her, she never failed to mention those of James Purdy and of Lancelot Law Whyte.

As I have said before, she regarded Whyte as one of the most potent influences in her life. We once went together to his Hampstead flat to pay the only social visit I ever made with her. The purpose of the visit was to look at some photographs he had taken of her hand holding a shell. She was so impressed by one that she had it reproduced as a Christmas card that year (1958) and, for the first and only time while I was with her, sent out cards to her vast list of acquaintances. This was done partly because she was proud of her hands— 'my hands are my face,' she often said—and partly to help Whyte, whose belief in a latent unity in which man sees himself as an integral part of nature, with his own feelings and thoughts as expressions of universal principles, matched what Allanah Harper described as her awareness of 'the interconnectedness of everything . . . the inclusion within the Divine Humanity of the whole creation'.

It was proof of Edith's affection for Whyte that she had accepted an invitation for afternoon tea, for by this time tea was a drink that 'bored the skirts' off her and the only cake that she could be induced to nibble was a macaroon. This predilection, she said, was a left-over from nursery treats, as was her liking for scrambled eggs and frankfurters, which was the meal she requested when she accepted an invitation from me.

Sunday was her rest day, in which she saw no one but her family and myself. So, on one particular Sunday in the autumn of 1958, I plucked up my courage and invited her to lunch with myself and some of her younger friends. I was both flattered and dismayed when she accepted. Money at that time was scarce and my flat was that rarity in London, a cheap and roomy one. The building itself, which was in a perilous state of decay, was tenanted mainly by Irish immigrants, who enjoyed nothing so much as a game of poker on the back lawn on Sundays.

With increasing apprehension I awaited the arrival of the big black Motor which, punctual as always to the minute, arrived outside the gateless entrance of what had once been an impressive Victorian façade. Never had the hall wall paper, drooping despondently above the entrance, looked more unappetising. The worn spots on the stair carpet became booby traps, menacing her approach; the banister appeared to shudder under her grip. I wondered nervously whether she would make the dangerous ascent in safety.

If Edith noticed anything at all her manners were too good to show it. Talking music with Gordon Watson and books with Michael Stapleton, she took a step at a time, leaning on her stick, her long fur coat falling back from the satin of her dress. If a sigh of relief escaped her as she sat in the one comfortable chair which my sitting-room boasted, it was camouflaged by her exclamations of delight at the sight of those two aristocrats, my Russian Blue cats.

'No, darling, it is not your mother I am wearing on my head,' she addressed the shyer of the two, who was regarding her fox-fur hat with suspicion. Like all true lovers of this most elegant and disdainful species, Edith waited for trust to be established before making overtures of friendship. She had not long to wait. By the time we had embarked on our frankfurters and scrambled eggs, cooked with Australian cunning by the fifth member of the party, Lorna Coates (referred to by Edith for some obscure reason of her own as Mumper), the bolder of the two was in her lap, consuming part of her sausage, offered by two delicate fingers.

Lunch was followed by recordings of some of her recitations of her own poetry. We listened to 'Most Lovely Shade' and to 'Still Falls the Rain'. When we came to the lines:

'The wounds of the baited bear,—
The blind and weeping bear whom the keepers beat
On his helpless flesh . . . the tears of the hunted hare'

I saw that she was weeping. She blew her nose vigorously.

'I always cry at that point when I am reciting. It is because of the bear, do you see? Osbert gets furious with me. "You are so damned sentimental about animals," he says.'

We changed the mood with 'Do Not Take a Bath in Jordan, Gordon', and she laughed with the same spontaneity as she had cried. Sipping our white burgundy, we made a circle around her, too absorbed to notice the volcanic explosions of sound that erupted into the room from the poker-players outside.

She began by explaining how 'The Little Ghost Who Died for Love', the poem dedicated to Allanah Harper, came into being. A poem, she said, very often has two 'fathers'.

'I saw a ghost when I was young. It was a face in a golden helmet on the Roman road that runs through Renishaw. Then years later I heard a Debussy quartet and it became the second father of the poem. Music fertilises me.'

Debussy and Ravel had become two of her favourite composers, but it had not always been so.

'When I first heard Debussy as a girl it upset me to listen to him. It was like having a squint. Then after a while I got used to it and I began to listen to him all the time.'

It was seldom that she talked about music without mentioning Stravinsky. She told us the story of a polka he had written as circus music, so rhythmic that it had started a stampede of the elephants.

From Stravinsky we moved on to Humphrey Searle, the composer who had set to music two of her major poems, 'Gold Coast Customs' and 'The Shadow of Cain', and who had introduced Gordon Watson to her when, as a young pianist, he had first arrived from Australia. She compared Searle's 'Gold Coast Customs' with Benjamin Britten's setting of 'Still Falls the Rain', remarking that they both showed 'an exact identity of feeling' with her. Gordon reminded her that Dylan Thomas, who had recited 'The Shadow of Cain' with her when it was performed at the Palace Theatre, had at first been unwilling to appear on the stage because he thought the sight of a little fat speaker would detract from its dramatic value—though, perhaps, add to its horror.

Edith laughed with us, but said that Dylan was the best male reciter she had known.

'He understood one's work, you see, which made such a difference. But oh, dear me, when it was over! We were all utterly exhausted. For four days I lay like a crocodile on the bank of a river, one hand upraised (as is their habit) in the hope of food being put into it but otherwise making no sign of life. In those days, you see, I had very little idea how to use my voice. It was Mr Stokowski who taught me how to produce it correctly.'

She told us that she preferred good bad music to bad good music, and similarly good bad people to bad good ones. One of her ancestors of whom she was very proud was the 'Wicked' Lady Cunningham who had stopped the flogging in women's prisons.

Her loathing of cruelty was inherited from both sides of the family. Her great-grandfather had found an escaped Negro living in a cave in the wood near his house. 'It was when they had slaves and the poor thing had run away from a sadistic master. He had killed a sheep in order to live which, in those days, was a crime punishable by death. My old boy bought him, refused to charge him and sent him back to the part of Africa from which he came'.

Michael Stapleton, who had undertaken the mammoth task of editing *The Queens and the Hive*, questioned her allegation that Queen Elizabeth was cruel in sparing the life of the deer but allowing their ears to be shorn off as ransom. He also pointed out that her picture of the 'soft and helpless creature, sobbing in its pain, rising upon the Judgement Day to confront her' was a contradiction of the teaching that animals have no souls.

Edith's answer was unhesitating: 'Michael dear, I am so grateful to you, and without your help the book would never get to the publishers, but I cannot change my opinion to suit anybody. Elizabeth may not have thought herself cruel, but it *was* hideous cruelty and to hell with the idea that animals have no after-life! What about what Christ said about not a sparrow that falls?'

By the time she left it was four o'clock, though the Motor had been ordered for three. After that first visit she came again and again. Oblivious of her surroundings, Edith felt the warmth of our affection and was at home in our midst.

In the autumn of 1959 came the last of our long trips in the Motor. She had written, earlier in the year, to tell me about it:

'I am to recite at the Edinburgh Festival on Wednesday the 9th September, in a huge theatre. I do hope you will come with me, will you?'

As the time drew near she began to plan the trip. We would meet at Sheffield and go the rest of the way by Motor, driven by a charming, intelligent, young local chauffeur. Outside Sheffield we would stop for lunch and she would bring egg sandwiches and wine. As always, she insisted that I should be accorded every luxury. I was to order all the morning papers to be delivered with breakfast to our respective rooms; I was to have my own bathroom, and supper was to await us on arrival. 'We shall want cold salmon, ham, a bottle of good white wine (not horrible cheap sweet stuff) and a large bowl of ice.'

The letter finished with a P.S. in red ink: 'Please, my dear, ask Mr Ponsonby's secretary to be *sure* I have a proper microphone.'

This was typical of her professional approach to any facet of her work. A wire I received shortly afterwards provided another example of this: it was also the one time she was openly angry with me. Because of last-minute alterations, I had been forced to have the poems for the recital typed elsewhere, where through carelessness on my part they had been typed in blue. The wire read: 'Impossible read ridiculous blue type. Please send clear black copies urgently. Edith.'

I apologised at once, but by the time I met Edith at the Sheffield station she had not only forgiven me but was overcome with remorse. Her irritability, she explained, had been born of fright. She had been terrified that she would be unable to see the blue type clearly by stage lighting. In a big hall it was essential that she read well in order to be heard. For this reason she rehearsed every word, posting various listeners at different points in the auditorium to be sure of audibility.

The curtain went up with Edith seated centre stage,

resplendent in purple and gold. Her cloak fell back behind her like a train, and around her neck was the gold collar which had been given to her by an American millionairess but which looked Aztec enough to arouse the interest of the British Museum. On the long hands she wore the famous aquamarines. Her appearance was greeted by applause, which she acknowledged with a perfunctory wave. She put on her glasses, picked up her typescript and began.

Unfortunately, the members of her audience were not as punctual as she was. Late-comers poured in, and the undisciplined rustle of chocolate boxes and programmes was interspersed with whispered 'excuse mes'. At last a voice was raised in the audience: 'We can't hear!'

At first Edith took no notice. She had told me on the way up that when she and Dylan Thomas recited in America there were always two deaf old ladies seated somewhere in the audience who complained because they could not hear. This was so regular that Dylan used to ask her before the performance where the afflicted pair would be found that night. Edith read on, her beautiful voice pitched on the level decided upon at the rehearsal.

Other voices informed her that they, too, could not hear.

Edith lowered her typescript and snapped at them: 'In that case pay more attention.'

'But we can't hear you.'

'Then get a hearing aid.'

There was a shocked silence. Round one had been won. Edith adjusted her glasses and began to read once more.

But the audience had not yet learned its lesson. Perhaps they enjoyed the unusual experience of provoking an artist, normally separated from them by the barrier of the footlights.

'We still can't hear,' they shouted.

This was heresy indeed. Edith lowered her typescript and removed her glasses.

'I have earned my living by reciting all over the world and if you can't hear me there is something wrong with you. I have no intention of ruining my voice to please you.'

In the silence that followed I could hear my heart thumping somewhere in the region of my throat. Edith picked up her typescript for the third time. A courageous member of the dress circle decided that here lay the explanation of the difficulty.

'If you lower your papers it would be better. Then we could see your face,' he suggested.

'You won't like it if you do see it,' Edith informed him.

I don't quite know what I expected to happen then—perhaps a riot of angry people demanding their money back. Panicking badly, I hurried back stage to instruct them to lower the curtain. When I told Edith about this afterwards she was more shocked than I had ever known her to be.

'Never do that,' she warned me. 'It is the one thing I could never forgive.'

Fortunately by the time I arrived back stage the audience had admitted defeat. They had also learned an important lesson. Not a sound came from anywhere in the auditorium. They paid her the compliment she had expected in the first place. They listened.

The newspapers, of course, had a field day. Every reporter in the building rushed to the telephone to wire the news to the evening papers. On the following day it received world coverage. What they did not report was the postscript to the story.

After the performance Edith remained in her dressing-room, chatting with Lord Harewood and Sir Compton Mackenzie who had come round to see her. It was almost an hour later before she drove back to the hotel and yet, waiting outside the stage door to see her go, was a crowd of between three and five hundred. They pressed round the Motor, close enough for me to see the expression on their faces. It was by no means just curiosity. They beamed affection and admiration, cheering her as she drove off.

'The Scots always like a fighter,' she said to me.

The fight took its toll, however, and on the way back to Renishaw her exhaustion began to show.

'All I want is to be left in peace,' she told me.

It was the one thing that never happened to her in all the years that I knew her.

Chapter Eight

THE EDINBURGH Festival of 1959 was the culmination of a year of activity. Heralded by her selection by Cliff Michelmore, producer of the programme 'Tonight', as the personality he most wanted to know, and reaching a high point with 'Face to Face', the John Freeman interview, it was a year of television appearances. It was also a year of recitals. There were two prior to Edinburgh: a reading of her own selection of poetry in the recital room of the Festival Hall, and a reading of her poem specially written for Benjamin Britten's concert in June. It was a year of recognition. Sir Maurice Bowra, giving the inaugural address as new President of the English Society, included Yeats and herself in his choice of Poets of Prophecy, as he had written to tell her he would. Her 'La Bella Bona Roba' received the Guinness Award for poetry. It was a year of hard work. Her Swinburne anthology was completed, and many of the poems for her collection *The Outcasts* were sent to be typed. *The Queens and the Hive* at last began to take on final shape. And it was a year of disaster. Her health, which had never been good, began to crack beneath the strain. Her letters to me were punctuated by complaints. 'I am half dead with fatigue.' 'My hand is agony,' and 'I have now got sciatica, which makes me terrified to move as my leg gives away.'

In spite of it, no challenge was allowed to pass unanswered, no opportunity was lost. The fighter battled on and nervous fatigue revealed itself in the irritability that crackled through the undiminished flow of her letters.

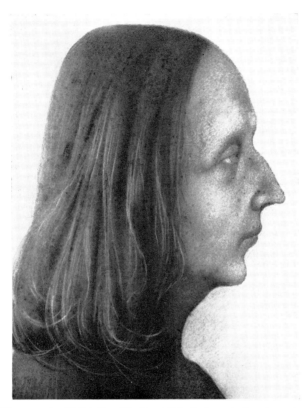

The portrait of Edith Sitwell by Pavel Tchelitchew, the Russian painter, which was hidden for thirty years behind a cupboard in her Paris flat

Edith Sitwell sightseeing with Pavel Tchelitchew in Toulon, 1931

The younger Edith Sitwell, 1937, after the publication of the favourite of her prose works, *I Live Under a Black Sun*

In the hat she wore at the Aldeburgh Festival, where we met. This photograph
pleased her because it made her look like a poet and not
'somebody's maiden aunt'

'My hand is my face', Edith Sitwell's Christmas card for 1958

Wearing her 'bird king's' hat at the 'Face to Face' interview, May 1959. She is telling John Freeman that if she were to appear in a coat and skirt people would doubt the existence of the Almighty

Edith Sitwell at the rehearsal of her 'Memorial Concert', 1962, wearing her
'Wages of Sin' (four aquamarines) and the 'Aztec' collar she
used for state occasions

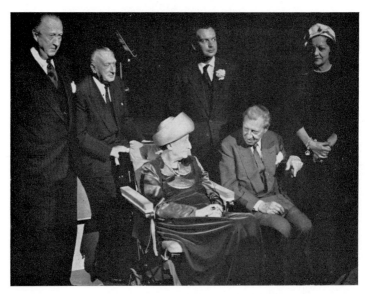

With her at the rehearsal, from left to right: Sacheverell Sitwell, Sir William
Walton, Francis Sitwell, Mrs Sacheverell Sitwell and, front right,
Sir Osbert Sitwell

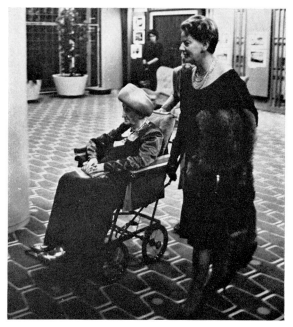

Edith Sitwell and myself at the performance of *Façade*, Royal Festival Hall, 1962

In the drawing-room of 42 Greenhill, N.W.3. From left to right: myself,
'Mumper' Coates, Edith Sitwell and Sister Farquhar

(The monument of Queen Elizabeth I in Westminster Abbey.) This could
have been Edith as she was when I saw her last

The first, which began on a warm personal note—'I did enjoy our meetings and look forward more than I can say to March'—continued as a tirade: 'I am almost a stretcher case from boredom over the enclosed preface for the Everyman book. Please, my dear, will you send it to Mr Bozman of Dents, tell him that I can now (which is true) hardly use my hand at all. And please tell the lady who asks me to lecture at the summer school that pressure of work makes it impossible. And return this appalling sketch to the Dane. Tell him I regret I cannot sign it as it bears no conceivable resemblance to me. I haven't got a face like a badly battered football.

'Life,' she wrote, 'is a week of Sundays in which a raging influx of bores has descended upon Montegufoni.' Her post brought her innumerable requests from reformers demanding her signature for their petitions.

'I am very worried. I told you that some parson wrote pestering me to sign my name to a petition asking that the law against homosexuality be changed. I have lost his address (he wrote from the official place from which they badger people and anyhow I don't know if I should sign it or not). I suppose I ought to do something about it (what a nuisance they are). I think of course that the law should be changed, but I do think it is a very nasty, messy subject. I could yell when I think of it. The parson must think I have nothing to do and ninety-six hours to his twenty-four.

'Canon and Mrs Collins pester me unremittingly. He on the subject of apartheid, never giving me time to answer yes before pestering me again, she to go and badger members of Parliament about the Atom bomb. If anybody else starts badgering me about sitting on platforms or going to Parliament, will you be an angel and tell them I have gone away for the winter never to return.'

Involved though Edith was with suffering humanity, it was the involvement of the artist, not of the social reformer. Politically she had a profound distrust of herself. 'I am incapable of understanding political questions,' she wrote. 'I was (I believe as well as hope) born to be a poet; and nobody can be that who does not care for great human problems. But I am unable to understand the mechanisms of politics.'

Poetry continued to be her solace and delight. In red ink,

to denote its importance, came a postscript to a letter which was the dawning of a poem she was later to dedicate to Father D'Arcy.

'My dear, will you please add this *wonderful* phrase that I have just found to my *Poet's Notebook:* "His Blood colours my cheek". St Agnes. Isn't it glorious?'

The first copy of her 'La Bella Bona Roba' arrived to be typed, and after my enthusiastic response she wrote: 'I'm glad you like the "Bella Bona Roba". I think it is one of the best poems I have written lately.'

The *Anthology* made its appearance at last and with it a major disappointment.

'I am ill with rage,' she wrote, 'about the *New York Times* review, though Osbert, who knows really far more than I do about reviews, says it is an excellent selling review—wonderful for the publishers to quote from and all the better because the reviewer, who obviously |hates my guts, has had to say the book is exciting—not once but twice.'

And later: 'I have just been insulted by the *Sunday Dispatch*. I suppose we shall never know why Ted Weeks sent them the *Anthology* but the creature who "reviews" in it gave it *ten lines* and all he could find to say was that Browning only got so many pages and Burns so many whilst Osbert and Sachie got fourteen. The compiler? Why, their sister, Dr Edith Sitwell (which doesn't happen to be my name).'

No wonder that, by Christmas 1958, she was 'out cold with a fearful headache'. In spite of it, she sent me a 'tiny present' and wrote at once when she had received mine.

A Christmas present for Edith to be sent to Montegufoni was a difficult assignment. I had settled on the unimaginative present of stockings for her and a dozen catnip mice for Savonarola. These are toy mice stuffed with herbs which attract cats and with which they will play for hours. The customs declaration read as follows:

For: Dame Edith Sitwell, D.B.E., D.Litt, etc. . . .
One pair stockings. One dozen toy mice.

'Oh how I laughed when I saw the customs declaration—toy mice!' she wrote. 'What can they have thought? It reminds me of when my great friend Bryher asked me to take through some flea-powder to her ex-husband in Italy for his cats. "And if the customs people ask you what that grey powder is, Edith, say, It is my flea-powder." Can't I say it is for Kenneth's cats, Bryher? I hardly like to say, "It is my flea-powder." "No, don't say that, Edith. They won't believe you and will think it is cocaine."'

The toy mice were a success and she wrote to say that 'Savonarola is mad about his pink mouseys. He dances and sings to them, leaving Nijinsky at the starting post with his leaps and levitations. He thinks Osbert is after them and so carries them about in his mouth for safety.'

Savonarola, who maintained her formidable name even after the secret of her sex was revealed, was a constant source of amusement: 'My lovely girl has been serenaded for a fortnight by eleven troubadours. While I was in bed, one troubadour followed her into the dining-room, whereupon she threw herself on to her back, shrieking and spitting until he was removed. I asked Osbert if he thought that Baby B. . . . [her name for a friend with a highly coloured reputation as well as an aversion to bath water] now perfuming the London air, threw *herself* on to *her* back when in the (alas all too frequent) same quandary. And he said, "Very probably!"'

Her letters accompanied a flow of work. The whole of *Atalanta in Calydon* was needed for the Swinburne Anthology; also 'Ave Atque Vale' and 'Sestina'. By January 21st ten chapters for *The Queens and the Hive* had arrived together with a manuscript of a new poem. The fact that Jean Cocteau had just sent her a drawing (the third he had done of her) may have had something to do with her renewed vigour. Although they seldom saw each other, her friendship with Cocteau meant a great deal to her. He was in the habit of sending her messages of admiration, sometimes accompanied by drawings, two of which she had framed and hung in her sitting-room.

'*Ce remerciement est venue de mon cœur qui vous aime (c'est à dire qui vous admire),*' he had written in 1955, after she had sent him a book of her poems; and later: '*Je peux rapprendre l'anglais de mes rêves et de mon enfance dans votre livre de poèmes. Les gens oublient que le génie existe . . . Restez ce que vous êtes et ce que nous émerveille.*'

As always, her correspondence was her chief source of stimulus and she continued to write to her friends, the same incidents appearing in each of her letters, told with the same careful amusing choice of words.

To Jeanne Stonor she wrote that she was 'just recovering from the most extraordinary visit—due to a misunderstanding—from the most frightful young man I have ever come across. He is Italian, speaks no known language but talks ceaselessly in a loud voice, is very vulgar, intrusive and inquisitive and has a head swollen to such a size that I can't think how he ever gets it inside any room. He is what Stephen Tennant used to call a "Bastille Bore", and it seemed at one moment as if we were going to be chained to him for life.'

To Gordon Watson she described a luncheon party she had attended because she was fond of her host and hostess, but which had not been a success:

'One man asked me if I enjoyed writing poetry! Before long I felt like the Duke of Gloucester, of whom it is reported that while in Cairo he was taken to a nightclub and there a hostess painted blue down to her cheek bones was presented to him. He stared at her speechless, then got a brainwave and said, "I say, do you know Tidworth?" So despairing!'

After a week's silence because of 'the worst sciatica I have ever had in my life—I shouldn't have thought such pain possible,' I received a description of a recital given in Florence.

'Just before I collapsed with sciatica, I gave a recital for the British Institute. After the recital people swarmed on to the platform. The ex-Ambassador of Holland; two young girls from Indo-China; the nice pretty young goose who is being painted by Annigoni; the Art Editor (! ! !) of the *Daily Express*, etc.

'When on dashed an enormous young man like one of those over-familiar, huge dank dogs that knock one down, and sucking my hand into one like a swamp in Florida, he pushed his face into mine and said, "You know who I am?" I said I didn't. He then said a name that I have never heard in my life and said, "My father says, do you remember sitting on his knee?"

'I drew myself up and absolutely *glared* at him. The ex-Ambassador drew nearer. The young girls from Indo-China stopped tittering. The Art Editor stared enthralled. The young man then added, as an afterthought, "As a child."

'I said, "I never sat on anyone's knee as a child, and I have never heard of your father." And turned my back on him.'

The letter contained a P.S.: 'The ex-Ambassador finally told the Consul that I reminded him, irresistibly and in every way, of Callas!'

In answer to a question I had asked about the poet Roethke, Edith sent this description:

'An immense man—he came to see me and promptly did a kind of strip-tease act, removing his coat, collar and tie. He then danced and recited, leaping forward in a most petrifying manner like a runaway horse. Twice he fell on his knees and once, burying his face in my lap, he began to weep convulsively. I said severely, "Mr Roethke, if you will get up, your tea is waiting for you." I caught him looking out of the 11th-storey window and back at my wrists to make sure that I would have no chance of holding him if he decided to jump. He roared and he chanted. Opinions differ as to what was the matter, some opining that he had been to too many parties, and was under the spell of the God. Two nights after this he rang me up at two-thirty a.m. begging me to give him a drug to make him sleep. I said I hadn't got any drugs, whereupon he sobbed into the telephone. After that he was whisked into a nursing home. A few weeks later he was out again and married.'

She had, she said, received 'yet another Song of the Earth'. She used to receive 'one a week from Nottingham', and in despair had decided to write one herself. 'I didn't see why I should be excluded from doing so by the fact that I am a poet, do you?' I repeat it from memory. This was Edith's 'Song of the Earth':

> 'Up the Workers,
> Use Tiz for tired feet,
> And there shall be no more corns
> Except the Workers' wheat,

Prefabricated houses shall be stronger
And holidays (if possible) even longer,
Only Russians shall have the Atomic bomb,
And Karl Marx shall be read in every home.'

When, at last, she had begun work again on *The Queens and the Hive* another interruption occurred.

'We had a really terrifying earthquake shock last night. I was dressing for dinner, had nothing on at all, when there was a sudden complete silence, then a rushing roaring noise such as I have never heard, a multiple crashing on the door that leads from my bedroom to the room where I keep my books. I could hear all the furniture being tossed about and then my bedroom began heaving about—sideways and back, up and down. I thought I was going to be turned upside down. It lasted for about five minutes. A new volcano had opened.'

Finally, in February 1959, just before she was due to leave Montegufoni for London, I had my first real indication of the nature of the furies which destroyed her peace and from which she fled. Her letters during the previous year had been punctuated by complaints such as 'I am being driven nearly frantic by the Income Tax people' and 'The Income Tax people are pestering me, set on, of course, by my television success.' When, to comfort her, I had told her about my own experience of double tax as an Australian living abroad, she had written at once to say, 'I am horrified to hear of the shock you have now had from the Income Tax people. It makes one feel quite sick when they go on like that. I suppose they are trying to depopulate the realm of all but the spies the Foreign Office hire to report their doings to Russia.'

As the Inland Revenue is a source of universal irritation to writers, I had not thought much about it. Not until a letter reached me, written in a hand which revealed the weakness of her condition, did I realise how deep-seated her anxiety was.

'I have been very ill indeed,' she wrote, 'though better today. For three days I couldn't keep any food down and got no sleep at all. The nights were an absolute nightmare of retching and a kind of mental horror. This was simply brought on by the Income Tax badgering me to send them money I have not got.'

This letter was, perhaps, the most significant I ever received from her. For the first time I understood that her life was lived on two levels. Her lavish hospitality, the size of her tips, her unfailing generosity, represented a *modus vivendi* born of habit. To live at all, she must live according to this pattern. If she had ever been capable of economising, which I doubt, she was no longer. Unable to restrain her own impulses, she was equally unable to escape the realisation of their consequences. Her growing debt under pressure from the Inland Revenue became a monster blown up into frightening proportions by the memory of her mother's disgrace. She had no weapon except her pride. Because of this she confided in nobody, not even her brothers. Only the impossible odds of sickness and despair made her seek an ally in myself. Her means of retreat were obvious. The brandy taken at night to calm her *angoisse*, the strong martinis beforehand and the liberal quantities of white wine that she drank with a meal were needed to relax taut nerves. Unfortunately, these were only temporary palliatives; in the long run both sickness and despair were accentuated.

It was obvious that something must be done to help her and it was this unhappy letter that provided me with an idea. In it Edith complained that 'not content with receiving an annual income that represents all my mother's money (which should have been one third of my income) Evelyn [Wiel] has got all my pictures and now won't come over to England, although I pay for everything, because, she says, she would have to get so many things. She really behaves as if she were Garbo.'

Ever since I had met Evelyn Wiel on my first visit to the Sesame Club, I had wondered how this strange old being could be so close a friend of Edith Sitwell. Now, at last, the explanation was given to me, for it was to Evelyn's flat, at 129 Rue St Dominique, that Edith had brought Evelyn's sister Helen Rootham, for the last years of her illness, and just before Helen died she had asked Edith to take care of Evelyn. The pictures mentioned were a collection of paintings by Pavel Tchelitchew bought by or given to Edith in the Twenties and Thirties.

When she came back from Italy in the spring of 1959, Edith asked me if I would go to Paris and bring back three of her favourite paintings. I was delighted to agree. My idea was to persuade her to sell her collection in order to settle her debts. Accordingly I set off for France in my battered little Austin sports car that had known better days, as we had agreed that it would be best to bring the paintings back with me.

The flat in Rue St Dominique, like the one at Pembridge Mansions, was on the top floor, and I climbed the seemingly endless flights of stairs in growing disbelief, trying to imagine an Edith capable of regarding them as part of the routine of living and even—according to her—carrying the *boîte d'ordures* up and down them during Helen's illness.

Poor old Evelyn Wiel was by now too deaf to hear her doorbell and so the door was ajar. I made 'my way through the shabby little corridor that led to the sitting-room embraced by a typical French balcony facing the Eiffel Tower. It looked what it was, a room untouched for thirty-five years. The wall-paper was peeling behind the cobwebs in the corners, the chairs hid their scars under cushions that alone had been re-covered. The aspidistra that was Evelyn's addition to the room stood dustily on the corner table.

Evelyn herself was waiting for me in the full splendour of her 'Paris personality', as she called it. This, she explained, was quite different from the Evelyn in London. Certainly her handsome face and beaming, toothless smile was more relaxed, though as indomitable as before. Lovable, charming, unscrupulously mercenary, she entertained me with the whisky that Edith had sent her. For the time being the purpose of my trip was forgotten, as, clad in Edith's clothes, her arms lined with bracelets that Edith had given her, her walls covered by Edith's pictures, she regaled me with stories of Edith's visits to Paris with Helen in those years before the war when she herself had been the wife of the Norwegian Consul.

Listening to Evelyn, I imagined Edith as she must have been when she first met Pavel Tchelitchew, in the days when she had visited Gertrude Stein and Alice B. Toklas and had met the artists and the writers of their *salon*.

Chapter Nine

—————⊃∘◯∘⊂—————

Nobody would have guessed at the
vulnerability concealed behind that mighty shield and buckler.
Stella Bowen on Edith Sitwell, 1927

FROM THE vantage point of old age, Edith could, in her
memoirs dismiss her years in Paris as 'unmitigated hell' and
for reasons already mentioned; Helen Rootham's death after
her protracted and agonising illness, and Edith's sacrifice of
poetry for prose in order to finance the costs involved.

None the less, listening to Evelyn Wiel, I began to understand that it was also a period of fruitful activity, growing
fame and encounters that were to lead to lasting friendships.
The most important of these was her meeting with Pavel
Tchelitchew, the Russian painter.

There can be no doubt, from everything Edith subse-
quently said to me, as well as what Evelyn told me that night,
that Edith was deeply in love with him. Their friendship was
a compromise which the artist in her recognised as inevitable
but the woman in her rejected and continued to reject until
his death in 1957. It was only a few months later that I met
her; the shock of it was still with her and she talked a great
deal about him.

'Artists should never marry,' she said to me. She believed
this to be true, particularly of herself, but the deprivation
was a sadness to her to the end.

When she first met him he was still a young man, some
years her junior. 'Desperately thin and desperately anxious-
looking', as she described him, he circled around her at the
première of the ballet that Sacheverell had written for
Diaghilev, staring at her. According to Edith this was because her features so closely resembled those of a friend of his

father that he was convinced she must be the grand-daughter, reputed to be living in Paris.

He was destined to paint her. 'I have an Englishwoman for Pavlik to paint,' Gertrude Stein told Stella Bowen, and shortly afterwards she introduced them to each other at her home at 27 Rue de Fleurus, in the studio lined with her famous collection of Matisse, Juan Gris and early Picassos. Miss Stein, described by Allanah Harper as 'filling her arm-chair with a voluminous cloth skirt covering her massive form, her magnificent head a mixture between a Roman emperor and an early Buddhist sculpture', was doubtful as to the outcome of her introduction.

'The fact that you have met Tchelitchew at my house does not mean that I will be responsible for him,' she warned Edith.

Perhaps she had seen the look of pleasure which, as observers afterwards noted, appeared on Edith's face in his presence. He was at his volatile best when he was with her, smiling the mischievous smile that lit up his mournful eyes, pirouetting around her and 'clapping his large painter's hands together' if something pleased him. Gertrude Stein, whom he described to Edith as the friend in Paris who 'understands me best and sympathises with me in my troubles and joys', probably understood these troubles well enough to see unhappiness ahead for Edith.

When Edith met him he was living 'in a little black hole of an apartment in the Boulevard Montparnasse', never free from money worries. The elder son of a Russian nobleman, he had been one of the many victims of the revolution. After enduring great hardship he had managed to escape to Turkey, where he finally joined a Russian travelling theatre who allowed him, in return for painting the décor, to sleep on the stage and share their limited food. By these means he arrived in Berlin, where he established the beginnings of his reputation as a painter and designer for the opera, attracting the attention of Diaghilev himself, whose promise of a ballet was the lure which had brought him to Paris. Jane Heap, editor of *The Little Review* in Paris, brought Gertrude Stein to see his work. Stein was impressed by what she saw, des-cribing it as 'the most mature and the most vigorous' of the group of young painters in Paris, with 'a distinctly new creative idea'.

Longing for the peace of the country, he accepted an offer from Stella Bowen of the cottage in which she and Ford Madox Ford had lived at Guermantes, a tiny hamlet thirty-eight kilometres from Paris. It was complete with garden and orchard and the rent was nominal, so that, even with his uncertain income, he was able to move with his sister Choura and his friend Allen Tanner and settle down there to paint furiously. Shortly after he met Edith, Diaghilev's offer of a ballet was realised and he went down to Monte Carlo to work on the sets. 'The subject of this ballet,' he wrote to her, 'of which the music has been written by Nabokov, a young Russian composer, has been taken from an ode by Lomonosov, a seventeenth-century Russian poet.' The whole effect was to be 'very grave and solemn—enough of this clowning with painted gauzes—people have forgotten that the stage is space and not surface, as they have tried to make us believe all this time. The only magician on the stage is the lighting—which has been too much neglected latterly.' His sets would dispense with the painted cloths which, he said, made the stage look like a *tableau vivant*, and use instead a cinema projection of pale geometric shapes on a misty blue background which would move in time to the music. It was a novel idea which he was afraid would shock Diaghilev. Diaghilev, however, although he had been ill in bed, appeared at a rehearsal smothered in plaids and coats, watched without comment until the end and then solemnly saluted Tchelitchew on both cheeks as a mark of approval.

Before he went to Monte Carlo Tchelitchew had painted his first portrait of Edith. 'I am very glad and very touched that you like your portrait,' he wrote to her. 'I am still rather anxious about it in spite of the fact that Gertrude Stein is pleased that you like it. She thought it a good likeness!' He was not so sure. 'I think I could do it better—I hope to be able to do so one day when you are in Paris for rather longer than the last time.'

As a painter he was fascinated by her. His love of the unusual attracted him to the woman, described by Stella Bowen as an 'English aristocrat, six feet tall, aquiline,

haughty, dressed in long robes and wearing barbaric ornaments,' and he considered her beautiful. To Alice B. Toklas,
in her *What was Remembered*, she was 'like nobody under the
sun. Very tall, rather the height of a grenadier, with marked
features and the most beautiful nose any woman ever had.
She was a *gendarme*. She wore double-breasted coats with
large buttons.'

Her clothes at that time must have given a somewhat
military impression. Amy Smart, a friend of her Paris days,
tells a story of French urchins pursuing Edith with shouts of
'*Soldat Anglais! Soldat Anglais!*' Edith turned on them with
great dignity and answered, '*Sans les soldats anglais vous
n'auriez pas gagné la guerre,*' and they slunk away,
vanquished.

Tchelitchew, however, rejected the '*gendarme*' both in
clothes and behaviour. He made it clear from the start that
he must be the dominant one in their relationship, storming
at her during one quarrel that she must '*ôtez les pantalons!*'
Outraged, she asked what he meant, and he informed her
that she must 'kindly leave the trousers to me and must stop
trying to be Joan of Arc, because it doesn't suit you and you'll
only be beaten.

'Two people,' he told her, 'could not rule.' When he
painted her he chose the most feminine of her dresses and
wrote to ask if she would get Helen Rootham to take a photograph of her in the dark-gold-patterned dress which he
liked so much, seated on her sofa so that he could see it to
the best advantage.

He was never tired of painting her: in mauve with her
'green-gold hair' shoulder length and 'the most beautiful
nose any woman ever had' well in evidence; in red with a
turban on her head; seated, with a pen in her hand, looking
every inch the poet. Six times he painted her and he did a
head in wax as well. Their relationship was stormy from the
beginning. On the occasion when he ordered her to *ôtez les
pantalons* she described him as yellow with rage, looking what
he said he was, *un tartare*.

'But,' he wrote to her, 'nobody has ever understood you
better, or come closer to you than I have and nobody ever
will,' and he assured her that theirs was 'a friendship that

has neither beginning nor end and which brings me enormous happiness and a limitless feeling of tenderness.'

The truth of this is apparent in his paintings, which she valued more highly than any of the many other portraits done of her.

As her visits to Paris were not of long duration, they got to know each other in those early years by correspondence, the greater part of which is deposited in an American university. But some of his letters she gave to me. From these it is apparent how much they had in common.

'One must recognise that all the truths of today are the old truths of yesterday,' he wrote. 'Those that weren't acknowledged, one might say, or that had not been noticed. It is very important that those truths that our predecessors haven't seen and accepted, being preoccupied by other ideas, should now be developed by us and made the heart of our researches. We must see something new in everything that we have usually despised.'

Surely this is only another way of saying what Edith said: 'We [the poets] . . . felt as if a physical world and its manifestations were a new reality. They must be examined as if we had suddenly burst into life.'

This longing for a new vision, for a re-awakening of creative force, appears again and again in his letters.

'I think something must happen, must break, and new, fresh forces fill the empty space left by all those people in whom we have put our hopes and who have deceived us with their pseudo powers and pseudo new discoveries. . . . Edith, we are asleep. We gently dream and we don't know what ought to be done. We must find new words, colours, forms, outside what has been already found and find them in places where people tread on them. . . . I wish some volcano would erupt as Etna has done—to break the hard, stupid shell of habit. I detest comfortable minds . . . I hate them. Do you understand me? Do you hear me?'

That she did understand him was clear enough. 'I am as sure of you as I am of myself,' he wrote later. 'The more I know you the more I become attached to you. I am sure you will write some wonderful poems, you who are too great even for your brothers to understand. . . . You have a superb

soul and a magnificent heart and I hope so much that nobody, not even your brothers, will make you do anything to
diminish your magnificent soul and heart. You are the spirit
and brain of the family. In fact there is only one Sitwell soul
and that is you. Don't be angry with me. I know, I have seen
it.'

Only from him would she have accepted this.

He spared her nothing of his self-doubt, his moments of
bleak despair, his isolation as an artist. He was particularly
conscious of the position of the foreigner in France.

'It is difficult to work here—it is a city which hates penni-
less foreigners. Paris is a magnificent city, but the French
worship money too much and they are idiotically patriotic.
I suffer enormously.'

An explanation of his lack of 'dominating creative power'
of which Gertrude Stein had begun to be aware can be
found in another letter in which he wrote: 'I am afraid to
look at pictures because they remain in one like nails and
one can't get them out of one's mind. . . . At the moment in
my work I am too much of a realist; everything seems an
unknown quantity to me so that I don't want to compose.
I don't want to make up my mind about anything.' And yet,
he continued, 'if one doesn't die of hunger this epoch is ideal
for painting because no one looks at what we do. We paint
pictures for ourselves and for the pleasure of our friends who
appreciate what we do, but we feel sad because of the isolation of what we do vis-à-vis society. Although a picture
and a book are material things, we are the makers of dreams
and of absolutely immaterial things which most people can
never see or understand. *Au fond* painting has not been appreciated in any age, but there were fewer painters and less fuss
in the past. We live at a time when everything is crumbling.
The crutches of Europe are collapsing . . . and we are good
for nothing in the eyes of the world.'

He was obsessed by the need to work, tormented when he
could not do so. 'I have started seven pictures in the last two
months, but have not finished one.' He begged her to write
to him, because 'There is sometimes such hell in my soul
that it is frightful to touch it, and you know that there isn't
a single person who can understand and console me more

than you.' If only she could come to Guermantes and be with him and his beloved sister Choura. 'We could be together, and read and work and laugh at things.'

This was never managed, although she visited him often at Guermantes, where they 'decorated the landscape', as Gertrude Stein put it. Here she would lie in the gaily coloured hammocks slung between the trees of his orchard, admiring the flowers he grew with such enthusiasm. Choura, whose frail health was a source of great concern to her brother, became a friend to whom Edith became attached, and who 'made the tragic, laughing, beautiful Anna Karenina a living human being for me'.

As always when she came upon what she regarded as great talent, Edith put her offers of help into practice, and used her widening influence in London to arrange an exhibition of his work at the Brook Street Gallery.

Over and over again he thanked her for the trouble she was taking to help him. Not only did she do the main part of the organising but she dealt herself with the pictures which he sent direct to her. Fifteen drawings, eight aquarelles, and seven gouaches went in one lot, with instructions to her to arrange for the gallery to supply the frames which would be bought only if the pictures were sold. He was to come to London for the exhibition, but not until the last moment, so that he was unable even to see to the last-minute difficulties.

The show was a success, and what with that and the excellent reviews of his ballet, Tchelitchew's name began to be internationally known and commissions for portraits poured in. Encouraged, he arranged for a *vernissage* at the Galerie Vignon, at which he asked Edith to act as hostess, as his sister Choura was too shy. Edith, ready as always to enlist help for him, wrote to Allanah Harper to ask her to be co-hostess. The *vernissage* would be followed by a joint party in honour of Pavlik on the same night.

Allanah Harper agreed, and the exhibition and the party attracted the élite of Paris. Pavlik, however, who found it difficult to accept help even from a close friend, was at his most temperamental. He left the party before the most eminent of the guests had arrived, and made a point of running away from any hint of possessiveness on Edith's part, although maintaining his own possessive attitude towards her. There were, no doubt, hurts inflicted on both sides; but she never stopped helping him as an artist, using the most unlikely occasions to bring his name before the public. One instance of this she described to Allanah Harper:

'The *Daily Express* has dragged us into a vulgar sordid murder. Headlines across a huge double-page spread read "Mystery Solved. Murdered man related to the Sitwell Family of Poets!" They had routed out the fact that my fourth cousin married as his second wife a woman who is sister to the murdered man's wife, from whom he had been separated for twenty years! . . . I gave the reporters absolute hell. I said, "How dare you come here and interrupt my work to ask me about a cock-and-bull story! You behave as though we were trapeze artists, not serious artists at all." They said, "Have you got a photograph of Mr X, Miss Sitwell?" "Has your editor got a photograph of Cain!" I enquired. "I don't understand," they said. "Then you shall. I am the same relation to X as your editor is to Cain, unless the Bible is wrong and Darwin is right, in which case he is descended from a monkey." Then I said, "You have come here to ask me about something ugly, but I will show you something beautiful" (and I showed them Pavlik's pictures). "You have dragged me into this ugly scandal; in return you shall please me by photographing these beautiful pictures and speaking respectfully of the great artist who painted them, in your paper!" And they have sent a photographer, so I am hoping they will do what I ask.'

She never ceased to believe in him, and in spite of the success of his later years considered that his greatness was never fully recognised. Her judgement was a good deal more constant than that of Gertrude Stein, who in the early days had encouraged him so greatly. 'Pavlik knows he can paint and he knows what he wants to do,' she had said of him, selecting him and Virgil Thomson as the only two artists in whom she believed. But, as time went on, she withdrew her favour. In her *Autobiography of Alice B. Toklas* she explains this: 'Gertrude Stein always says to the young painters when they complain that she changes her mind about their work. It is not that I change my mind about the pictures, but the paintings disappear into the wall, I do not see them any more and then they go out of the door naturally.'

This was a blow to Tchelitchew, who was convinced that mischief-makers had been at work. His affection for Gertrude Stein turned to resentment. Fortunately Edith, though influenced by him as an artist, was not so affected by his opinions and her friendship with Gertrude Stein survived. In the words of that lady: 'This friendship like all friendships has had its difficulties but I am convinced that fundamentally Gertrude Stein and Edith Sitwell are friends and enjoy being friends.'

It was Stein's book, *Geography and Plays*, that brought them together. Edith, who had reviewed it for the *Athenaeum* in a moderately enthusiastic manner, spent some months studying Stein's style and wrote an article for *Vogue* which began, 'In the future, it is evident that no history of the English literature of our time could be of any worth without a complete survey of the work Miss Gertrude Stein is doing for our language. She is, I am convinced, one of the most important living pioneers.' This appeared in October of 1925 and shortly after that Miss Todd, the editor, arranged for Edith to meet Miss Stein. 'Withdrawing and hesitatingly advancing', Edith entered the studio, and both writers being fascinated by each other's work, Edith became a frequent visitor to the house at 27 Rue de Fleurus. The conversation, according to Miss Toklas, remained almost exclusively on the subject of literature. Stein considered that Edith had the mind of a man, and Edith that Stein was bringing life back to language that had become 'a threadbare thing, too tired to move, breaking down the predestined groups of words and their sleepy family habits and rebrightening their use by building them into fresh shapes'.

So their acquaintance flourished, and with Miss Stein Edith met many of the artists of her day, including Pablo Picasso. It is worth mentioning, however, that, though both writers were renowned for their sense of fun—'We are not serious because we are serious,' Gertrude Stein wrote to Allanah Harper—Edith never showed this side of herself at 27 Rue de Fleurus. There they admired her for her poetry, liked her as a person but did not discover her wit.

Such a friendship between two such famous experimenta-
lists did not go unremarked, and Sylvia Beach of the Shakespeare and Company Bookshop decided to bring the two of
them together in public by inviting Edith to lecture on the
subject of Gertrude Stein. Unfortunately, due to a misunderstanding between Sylvia Beach and herself, Edith gave a
reading of her own poetry instead, an occasion described by
Natalie Barney for *Adam*, in the *International Review* of 1962:
'Edith sat majestically remote above her audience. Her
long Elizabethan hands, bearing no papers, met in their
virginal loveliness, sufficient unto themselves. . . . She rose
to read, but what were those strange un-Steinian rhythms now
scanned by this unique poetess's lips? Were they not some of
Miss Sitwell's own?'

As Edith continued, Gertrude Stein's expression became
forbidding. 'She sat bolt upright, meditating, in spite of a
twitch of her hands, a more gentlemanly reprisal than immediate exposure.' When drinks were handed round later
in the evening, Miss Barney 'perceived with awe that Gertrude Stein had gone home. So no toasts followed, nor indeed
were any *de circonstance*, lest they come from embittered lips.'

It was a misunderstanding which Edith was to hold against
Sylvia Beach for the rest of her life. Time, however, healed
the breach and Miss Toklas, whom I saw recently in Paris,
summed up her own and Gertrude Stein's opinion of Edith
as 'completely attractive in every way'.

For Stella Bowen, another close personal friend of those
days, 'the most extraordinary thing about Edith Sitwell is the
big gap that exists between her quite wonderful but alarming
façade and the soft and flagrantly human woman it conceals.'

This warm-hearted Australian-born painter with 'the gift
of admiration', as her agent Mrs Bradley put it, acted as
mediator in those early days of Edith's friendship with
Tchelitchew. She understood their similar temperaments,
their artistic *rapport*. Although Tchelitchew could not at this
stage read English, he 'saw' Edith's poetry in the same way
as she did herself. 'The shape and texture of Edith's words
were like surfaces felt by the fingertips,' Stella Bowen wrote.
With her they discussed the work they planned together,
a book, and—a suggestion on his part—an opera. She en-

couraged their friendship, understanding its value, for she wrote to Edith, 'He really is a very special person. I think we do well to cherish him, in spite of his many short-comings.'

To Allanah Harper, Edith owed her discovery of Rainer Maria Rilke, as she first read a poem of his in Allanah's review *Echanges*. She wrote an enthusiastic response:

'It is superb. Do tell me something about him. Arthur Waley, to my great distress, tells me he is dead, which is a real grief to me, because he is a great poet. I can't tell you how excited I was when I read that poem.' In a later letter she added: 'Some time I intend to do a poem in English on one of the themes in Rilke's poems. Don't you think it would be an interesting thing to do?'

Grateful for the encouragement that Allanah Harper was giving to contemporary poets by publishing their work, Edith described her as one of the people who see 'the continuity of the great tradition in the poets of today, which they enrich with new technical experiments which become a part of the unbroken chain of the poetry of the world.' . . . 'You understand,' she said to her, 'that the artist does not imitate things in nature, he creates with the Creator new forms and new things.'

With Allanah, Edith met the literary and artistic world of Paris. It was a world of *salons*, such as the Duchesse de Rochefoucauld's; gatherings dedicated to one of the arts, at which Edith met Sir James Frazer, author of *The Golden Bough*—a meeting that was not a success, as Sir James talked mainly about the Paris underground, how it smelt and how he was constantly being assaulted by middle-aged Parisiennes —and was introduced to contemporary painters and writers such as Marx Ernst, Tristan Tzara and St Jean Perse, James Joyce and Paul Valéry.

*   *   *

This, then, was Edith's Paris in those early days before her world became narrowed to the confines of Helen Rootham's sick-bed, before the 'silent presence', as Amy Smart described it, 'was forever next door preventing laughter and exuberant conversation.' The flat at 129 Rue St Dominique remained a shrine to these memories.

Although it could not be said that Evelyn had 'looked after' them, Edith's possessions had been guarded by the fierce old woman against the German invaders and the letters from which I have quoted and which Edith later gave to me were among the personal possessions now gathering dust on the shelves. It seemed to me as I stood on the little balcony overlooking the Eiffel Tower that the twenty-five years since Edith herself had stood there were denied by the dusty apartment. Her books were piled on the mantelpiece. The main part of her collection of pictures was stacked against the wall of the small room that had been Edith's bedroom. The sight of them brought me back to the purpose of my visit and I asked permission to look at them. There were more than I had expected and their condition seemed to me to be remarkably good considering that they had been so badly neglected.

I returned to London, armed not only with the three pictures that Edith had requested, but with the hope that my idea might prove to be more beneficial than I had first imagined.

PART II

The Beginning of the End

Chapter Ten

If I'd been Chinese I should have been exposed on the mountains with my feet bound.
Edith Sitwell to John Freeman in *Face to Face*

I CAME BACK from Paris to find Edith Sitwell a household name. 'Face to Face', the television programme in which she was interviewed by John Freeman, had been shown the night before and first proof of its effect was the reaction of the customs officer who checked the paintings I had brought back with me. Like most travellers, I am familiar with this species—stony-eyed men whose polite, set faces manage to convey that you are guilty until proved innocent. At the mention of her name, this one was transformed.

'Dame Edith Sitwell! Oh yès, I know her. Saw her on telly last night. Quite a character, isn't she!'

As I drove off, I reflected that this is the Englishman's seal of approval. Although anxious himself to hide behind a uniformity of clothing, habits and clichés that make the language as comfortable as well-worn shoes, he appreciates above all else a 'character' who refuses to conform.

Hugh Burnett, producer of 'Face to Face', told me that when the programme was first devised, they were on the lookout for such 'characters'—controversial personalities of universal interest—with the idea of converting them before the cameras into the people they really were. Edith, one of the first three on their list, was more successful than they had dared anticipate. As John Freeman put it, in his introduction to the re-play of 'Face to Face':

'The producer and I thought that this programme was going to be a sympathetic study of an eccentric poet. Dame

Edith turns out to be far more than that, a natural, generous and sometimes very funny human being.'

She was at her ease with him because, she said, she enjoyed talking to him. 'The most exciting and formidable talker' that John Freeman had ever met, answered (or refused to answer) his questions as she would have done in her own drawing-room, committing every kind of heresy in the process and emerging triumphant.

Tackled first about her appearance, she demolished her critics with the observation, already quoted, that if she were to appear in a coat and skirt, people would doubt the existence of the Almighty. She claimed her Plantagenet ancestry with a pride that was offset by a later statement that she was a worker who had known great poverty and who worked regular hours each day. She informed millions of viewers that her mother had been forced to marry her father at the age of seventeen, and that neither of them 'knew much about life'. She confessed, without shame, to a loathing of country walks, or indeed exercise of any kind, and denied having sought publicity except when she had refused 'to be taught her job by nincompoops'. She also denied adamantly that she was a member of the Establishment, but admitted to enjoying intensely the honours being showered on her. Although she had friends, she said, from all walks of life, she was a 'forbidding old lady' in whose presence no young person would dare to misbehave. Finally, after proclaiming her admiration for America and Americans, she ended on a declaration of faith. 'The Great Fire' that broke out of her into poetry was, she said, 'a humble but unworthy love of God and of humanity'.

In other words Edith was, very simply, Edith. For the first time in her life, ordinary people were given the chance to see her undistorted by press reports and the caricaturist's pen, and they liked what they saw.

Hugh Burnett had arranged for Feliks Topolski to draw her so that his sketches could be shown on the screen before her appearance. So, for the last time in her life, she sat for an artist, visiting him at his studio under the railway arch of Hungerford Bridge. She did not, however, enjoy the results, which she described as 'unspeakable caricatures'. The royal effect of the crown he gave her to wear was offset by the curvature of her spine which, she said, was stressed to make her look like a hunchback. A press report added fuel to the fire by reporting that Topolski was also painting the young poet Christopher Logue, as he considered it amusing to represent both the young and old in poetry at the same time. Since a few weeks previously Edith had been 'obliged to rebuke *The Times* and the *Daily Mail* for announcing that poor Mr Christopher Logue's egregious performance of his verses coupled with jazz is a new art form,' she was not best pleased. His combination of poetry and jazz, she told Pamela Hansford Johnson indignantly, was 'not a new art form and it did not originate in San Francisco but was pinched from the idea of my *Façade*, which was first performed thirty-seven years ago.' To compare the two, she said to me, was like 'comparing the winner of an egg-and-spoon race with the winner of the Greek Olympics'.

Logue defended his claim by pointing out that whereas Edith had recited her words from behind a gauze veil, he had spoken into a microphone; that she had used dance music where he had used jazz. Edith remained unconvinced at the time, but later both feuds were resolved amicably.

As Edith's physical strength decreased, public demands on her time became greater. In addition, the private load of money worries that she was still carrying began to invade her sleeping hours. The result was exhaustion that led towards total collapse.

'Poor worn-out electric hare that I am,' she said, 'I have been pursued relentlessly by greyhounds in the shape of television producers and journalists.' Her fatigue was such that it was giving her 'an alarming mixture of megalomania and inferiority complex'.

Fighter that she was, little or no hint of this appeared in public. Life continued much as usual, except that, to the keen observer, it became noticeable that though Edith's fork was lifted to her mouth with the same regularity as anybody else's, when her plate was taken away most of the contents remained untouched. There was nothing one could do about it. 'Fussing', as she dismissed it irritably, was forbidden. 'There are moments,' she said, 'when I feel it would be better to retire into a lunatic asylum. I don't mind people saying they are the Emperor of China, but I *do* mind non-stop fussing.'

She continued to fulfil her social and public obligations, partly out of habit and partly to make money, and in the following month she appeared, for the second time, on 'The Brains Trust'. This programme she would have done well to avoid. The very qualities which in 'Face to Face' had led to an outstanding success, told against her in a Brains Trust. The most subjective of women, she was capable of drawing any audience into the orbit of her personality and of holding them captive, but she was unable to make objective pronouncements on issues that lay outside it. It may be that poetic genius implies an intensity of interest and appreciation that must have boundaries in proportion to its depth. As a poet Edith was not, she said to me, 'attracted by that kind of poetry which seems to me the expression of ideas and feeling that are not born from poetic genius. Poetry should be born from this as music should be born from musical genius.' Nobody was truer to this concept of poetic genius than she was. In these last years of her life political or social questions could not interest her unless they touched her emotions. She was a formidable and exciting talker because she could magnetise any conversation towards herself. Put Edith on a quiz programme and she would have been lost.

One question, for instance, she was asked on 'The Brains Trust' was: what would she do if she happened to be a pedestrian crossing a road (which she never was) and a man threw a cigarette packet out of a passing car? She replied that, whatever she felt, she would be too much of a lady to show it—an answer that was designed to amuse, but which had no bearing on the subject whatsoever. Because she was at a disadvantage, the faults in her personality were exaggerated like the lines of her face under the cameras. She was sufficiently the performer to know that she had not appeared at her best, but the programme did not interest her enough for her to mind.

Then just before she was due to set off for Montegufoni in November of that year, 1959, she had the first of the frightening series of falls which were to lead her towards the wheel-chair in which she spent the last three years of her life.

It happened on the night before a giant tea party in honour of the young poet David Lutyens, descendant of the famous architect and a devotee of hers. Around midnight my telephone rang and Edith's faint voice came from the other end:

'My dear, I'm so sorry to disturb you, but I have had an accident. No, I'm not injured, except for a lump the size of an ostrich egg over my right eye. I'm lucky to have the sight of it.'

Her bed, which she described with more feeling than accuracy as 'broken in three parts and lightly bound together with string', and which was, in fact, propped up by telephone books at one end, had collapsed. According to her own account she had been precipitated on to the floor and had struck her forehead on the corner of the bedside table. She was perfectly all right except for the fact that she was 'black and blue down to the base of my throat'.

This was no exaggeration, as I found when I went in to see her next morning. But Edith, whose inherited tendency towards hypochondria had magnified every ailment she had ever suffered, when really afflicted was really brave. She was much more concerned about the party and the awful task I would have in putting off nearly one hundred people in the few hours left. In the end, she insisted that I should act as hostess myself.

Her tea parties were a left-over from the days when she entertained every Saturday at Pembridge Mansions and justified the opprobrium they received from her close friends. They were an anachronism that only a hostess of her drawing power could perpetuate. Her luncheon parties and cocktail parties did, at least, give people some chance of talking to her: at her tea parties they had almost none. Guests were handed tea and sandwiches, led up one by one to be presented and forcibly moved out of the way when the next guest arrived. It was then up to me to see that they talked to each other and drank their tea until such time as Edith read a poem or, if she was unable to read herself, played a recording of her poetry, or perhaps the Yeats record in which he discussed her work. Because she was Edith Sitwell, people came and were glad to do so. Without her, as Mrs Louis Kentner said on this occasion, it was a case of *Hamlet* without the Prince. I did what she asked, however, and played the part of hostess, and it speaks well for the good manners of her guests that it was no more of an ordeal than it was.

Soon afterwards, still badly bruised and with the lump still the size of an ostrich egg, she embarked on the two-day train trip to Montegufoni, shrouded by a hat with a tall crown and a heavy black veil that came to be known as her witch's hat. Only Edith could have worn it and only Edith could have faced that trip so soon after her fall. Then, before the winter was out I received a letter written flat on her back:

'You will hardly credit it, but I have had another really frightful accident, brought on simply by the fact that, since the accident in London, I have been frightened to be in complete darkness.

'On Wednesday at about 1 a.m. the light near my bed went out. I got out to try and find the light near the door. Then, thinking I had found my bed, I caught hold of a chair, which went down and I crashed on to the base of my spine. I had to lie on the floor with no blankets and no pillows till I was called. I was then lifted on to my bed, screaming with agony. I can't sit up or move.

'The doctor is coming tomorrow. I didn't send for him before because I simply cannot stand non-stop fussing on top of really fearful pain. I couldn't have believed such pain existed.'

By the time the doctor came, a metamorphosis had taken place. She charmed him, she amused him; he accepted her own belittling of her condition and went away convinced that she was well on the way to recovery. I was to witness this performance over and over again in the course of the next years. It made the job of looking after her a great deal more difficult, but, knowing Edith, it was impossible to blame the innumerable doctors who were thus deceived.

In fact, she was far from recovery. The next months brought a gradual worsening of her condition until, finally, she was forced to go into hospital in Sheffield. Three weeks later she returned to Renishaw, but shortly afterwards she had fallen again and broken one of the frail bones of her wrist.

Her family, worried about her health and anxious for her safety, were faced with the choice of either installing a nurse at Renishaw or further hospitalisation for Edith. They decided on the latter and booked her into a London nursing home. But they had reckoned without Edith. She sent me a wire asking me to meet her at the Sesame Club and informed me that, as her health no longer permitted her to travel, she would remain permanently in London.

We met, I remember, in the foyer. She had on a close-fitting feather hat that was slightly askew from her long car journey from Sheffield. Above the pallor of her cheeks, purple smudges showed like bruises under the eyes. Her wrist was still in plaster and her movements revealed the extent of her fatigue. It was obvious that she should have been in bed, and obvious, too, what her future must be. In a wave of that protective sympathy to be felt by so many others in the years to come, I told her that she could count on me. I knew as I said it that, for a spirit too arrogant, too courageous, too obstinately alive for her body, the struggle ahead would be a fierce one. There was no doubt that, to win it, she was going to need her friends.

Chapter Eleven

————⊃∘◯∘⊂————

When I die I will be able to say that
I've given more devotion and had more devotion than most people I know.
Edith Sitwell to John Freeman in 'Face to Face'

THE ONE factor guaranteed to take Edith out of herself was a friend who could interest her. This qualification is necessary as, although her circle continued to widen, not all her friends had the power to do so.

Among those who had were Pamela Hansford Johnson and her husband, then Sir Charles Snow. Edith had read their work and admired it, and there was an additional link through Pamela's close association with the youthful Dylan Thomas.

As Constantine FitzGibbon points out in his biography, Thomas had been noticed by Stephen Spender and others before his *25 Poems* appeared in 1936, but it was Edith's favourable review that brought him into focus as a poet of importance. It roused a storm of controversy which occupied the *Sunday Times* correspondence section for some weeks. The main outcry was against his obscurity. 'Clarity,' as one correspondent expressed it, 'is a perennial characteristic of all great poets. . . . I concede that poetry will never appeal to the plain "man in the street". It should, however, appeal to the man in Intellectual or Beautiful street.'

Edith, never loth to take up a challenge, sent back a spirited reply, to the effect that the argument seemed to be developing into a beauty competition. Her letter finished with the tart comment that if she wanted to be taught her job by somebody who wrote for *Poetry Review*, she would send in a request, but that she would as soon ask a writer in the *Poultry Gazette* to teach her to train eagles to fly.

From this it will be seen, as in all her literary battles, that she more than held her own, but she had another champion for her cause. One of the few letters printed in Dylan's defence was by the youthful Pamela Hansford Johnson, then a girl in her twenties. It was a clear-sighted, vigorous assessment, followed, a year or so later, by an equally perceptive review of Edith's 'I Live Under a Black Sun', which she described as a 'passacaglia having such subtle counterpoint, such rare decoration, that it should urge still further her acceptance as the most unique musician in literature of our time'. It was a description that would have greatly pleased Edith herself, but ironically enough, she never saw it. 'How much it would have meant to me if only I had seen your review of my *Black Sun*,' she wrote to her. 'I only saw one by Wilfred Gibson and by the late lamented (but not by me) goosie gander Dr Edwin Muir, who said the book had no point and he didn't know what it was about.'

She had, however, read Pamela Hansford Johnson's novels, and had once given me *An Avenue of Stone* because, she said, 'Women novelists at their best have a peculiar insight and sensibility, added to passion, which differentiates them from the male insight and sensibility.'

This, then, was the background to a letter to Edith which arrived one day from Sir Charles Snow. His reason for writing, he said, was a novel which his wife had just finished and which had been suggested by the closing years of Frederick Rolfe's life.

'In the course of her book,' he wrote, 'the "hero", whose name is Skipton, runs across a literary group who are visiting Bruges. The centre of this group is a woman of forty called Dorothy Merlin. This woman is not an amiable character, either seen objectively or through Skipton's paranoiac vision. She is an Australian with seven children: she writes verse-dramas (bad) mainly about having seven children: she gives lectures for the British Council: and the only work of art she knows about, except her own, is *Kristin Lavransdatter*.

'To our horror, it has just been suggested to us that some readers might think my wife was intending a malicious parody of yourself. I don't think any suggestion I have ever

[126]

heard has ever surprised me quite so much. I have tried to forget the true origin of this character, and have searched point by point for facts that (a) she is a strong personality (b) she inspires some hero-worship, but I can see not one. She is a bad playwright while you are a major poet; she is an Australian housewife, and you are an aristocrat. She doesn't admit the existence of any other writer, while we have all seen the proofs of your generosity. And so on, in every psychological and physical detail.

'But both my wife—who is ill at the moment or she would have written to you herself—and myself are distressed even by the suggestion. The literary life is full enough of pinpricks without causing more, however innocently, to those one respects; if there were anything in the book you didn't like my wife would wish to cut it out. Have you time to cast your eye over the typescript? I know it is an infliction to put extra work on to you and we wouldn't think of asking you if we were not bewildered.'

After a few days of enjoying the joke and, no doubt, thinking out an answer—I know, from studying her manuscript books, how carefully she prepared letters which she regarded as important, sometimes copying them out in full before deciding on a final draft—Edith replied as follows:

Dear Lady Snow,

How much I laughed when I received Sir Charles' letter.

I am, at the same time, alarmed, for I am at the moment finishing a book called *The Queens and the Hive* which is about Queen Elizabeth I and Mary Queen of Scots and contains a rousing account of Catherine de Medici planning the massacre of St Bartholomew's Eve. I am now terrified that this may be supposed, by any readers I may have, to be a lascivious portrait of you. After all, you are not Italian, do not persecute Protestants, and are not the mother-in-law of Mary Queen of Scots, so the likeness springs to the eyes!

What do you suppose I have done with my seven offspring? Eaten them?

Nonsense apart, it is an ill wind that blows nobody any

good. I am a very great admirer both of you and of Sir
Charles and have longed, for ages, to know you both.

And now I shall!

What is more I shall have the privilege of reading your
new book before it comes out. I look forward to it more
than I can say.

I am sorry you are ill and sympathise deeply. I had
Asiatic influenza twice before Christmas and still feel
the effects, have also had gastric flu and have recurrent
migraine.

If you do, by any happy chance, feel better, how delighted I should be if you would accompany Sir Charles to
luncheon with me on Tuesday. But people will pester one
when one is ill, so I don't.

With warm admiration,
yours sincerely,
Edith Sitwell.

The letter finished with a characteristic P.S.:

'Do you think it would help if I put a note in my book:
"The portrait of Catherine de Medici is not meant as a
portrait of Miss Pamela Hansford Johnson"?'

The manuscript, *The Unspeakable Skipton*, was duly read
by Edith and pronounced Pamela's finest work. On the
appointed day they arrived for luncheon.

Because of the bizarre introduction to the guests of honour,
I remember this particular party with unusual vividness.
Conversation got off to a good start with the discovery of a
common enemy, none other than the Cambridge don who
had asserted that Edith 'belonged to the history of publicity':
Dr F. R. Leavis.

Edith, who enjoyed her enmities almost as much as she
enjoyed her friendships, had engaged in a running battle with
Dr Leavis for many years. Dr Leavis, like Wyndham Lewis
before him, must have discovered that to tweak her tail
through the bars was a dangerous proceeding. As I hope I
have shown, Edith's resentments were easily enough banished.
When they were not, her antagonists became the objects of
unmerciful teasing, and Dr Leavis had, for many years,

headed the list. While I was with her she had an especially persistent 'pest' with delusions of grandeur. Demanding back a magazine he had sent her, he informed her that unless it was returned he would insist on the Queen personally directing the search for it. If this failed he would appeal to the Pope. Edith wrote herself to tell him to send everything to Dr Leavis and not to be discouraged if he did not answer, but to persevere until he did. From Chicago, 'aided and abetted,' she told us, 'by my young friends there', she sent on to Dr Leavis an invitation she had received from a local quack healer. It was headed, 'O Noble and Esteemed One', and contained the sentence, 'Our girls wait only to hold you in their arms.' When she came to write her memoirs, her attack on Dr Leavis began, 'He has a transcendental gift, even when he is writing sense, of making it appear nonsense.'

Her meeting with the Snows happened well before Dr Leavis's much publicised attack on C. P. Snow, but he had already made his antagonism felt. On this occasion, critics, generally, were the subject of conversation. She told a favourite story about Lincoln Kirstein, 'a simply enormous American friend, who, leaning suddenly towards an art critic talking about painting, said "Oblivion awaits you". After which there was silence.' Sibelius had said to her brother Sacheverell, 'A statue has never yet been erected to a critic', but one critic, 'a poetaster of no talent,' had recently had the temerity to bring out a book of poems. 'His wretched little verses have the dimensions of a pre-fabricated house— airless and stuffy. And the paper for which he wrote is pro- ducing the most arrant, abysmal bosh. The leading article has to be seen to be believed. It says we can all write poetry if we are sensitive enough! All we need to do, apparently, is to wince incessantly. I knew Mr Yeats, who was very kind to me, Tom Eliot, Wystan Auden and I knew Dylan. None of them ever winced in *my* presence!'

By *Lolita*, an early copy of which she had been sent from America, she confessed herself to be horrified. 'The first pages,' she said, 'are sad and idyllic like Annabel Lee—but cruelty and the corruption of children are the two things that shock me most. There may be something in it I don't see. But how can people think it funny?'

No Bail for the Judge, by Henry Cecil, she pronounced
'wonderfully funny', and it was this book that led to a friendship between herself and the Cecils. It was sealed by the
Battle of the Noise.

In spite of her weakened health, those early months of
residence at her club had been bearable. But fate was against
her. The building next door was to be converted into office
premises; floors were being removed and walls knocked
down. Edith's bedroom adjoined the dividing wall.

The news was broken to me by a distracted phone call from
Edith, earlier than usual, announcing that the people next
door had taken to throwing their furniture around so that it
was impossible for her to work. By the time I arrived at
twelve-thirty the hammering had given her a headache and
the electric drill had made her bedroom shake so much that
she was afraid for her possessions.

Used though I was by now to crises, this one floored me.
The ordinary noise of London club life had already begun
to prove too much for her, and the clatter of conversation
in the dining-room irritated her. 'Quack, quack, quack—
and it isn't as if they have anything interesting to say,' she
would complain, glaring fiercely at her offending fellow-
members.

More noise, I knew, would try her over-strung nerves to
breaking point; and this is what happened. Because she was
already exhausted, her sense of proportion deserted her. She
regarded the conversion as a personal assault on her
sensibilities, designed to force her out of her club. Neither her
doctor nor myself could persuade her otherwise. For her it
was a hostile force, to be fought and subdued. The 'alarming
mixture of megalomania and inferiority complex' was beginning to reveal itself.

'They are not going to make me move out of my room,'
she declared. 'Who do they think I am? Do they imagine I
would go away to please them?'

It was an unreasonable attitude that caused immense
damage to her nervous system. Three months of constant
hammering and drilling left her with a disease of the middle
ear. Her appetite went altogether and she began to depend
on brandy and milk for her nourishment. But Edith did not

budge, and her resistance made the comparatively trivial matter of a professional firm moving into the premises next door into one of national concern. I wrote letters to the contractors and to the managing director of the firm in question. She called upon the Noise Abatement Society, the press, the police and even the Prime Minister. And she ultimately called upon her new friend, Henry Cecil.

John Connell, the secretary of the Noise Abatement Society, was anxious to help, delighted at so famous a recruit to his cause, but things went from bad to worse. One Saturday afternoon, she rang Scotland Yard. 'If you don't tell the workmen to stop I shall have to go round there myself at eight o'clock on Monday morning and slap each one of their faces in turn,' she informed a startled constable at the other end. She retailed his reply to me with some amusement: 'In that case, Madam, we shall be forced to restrain you.'

Finally John Connell marshalled the press, and, as she told me next morning, 'At seven o'clock last night, when you were not available, my dear, reporters in a long procession telephoned me saying that Mr Connell and a Comus rout are descending upon me this morning to join me in signing a document telling the workmen next door to cease upon the midnight with no pain.'

I hurried round to the club to find the 'Comus rout' in full force. Lord and Lady Foley, who were fellow sufferers living near by, and who had promised to join her, had been barricaded into their house by the press. By the time I got there the foyer of the Sesame Club was filled with reporters and photographers.

Edith informed us that she was 'for the first time in sympathy with the Duke of Windsor, who was reported to have used a word to the press photographers that he must have got out of *Lady Chatterley's Lover*.' In due course they disappeared and the results of their visit appeared on the front pages of the popular press.

The noise, however, continued. The contractors arranged to give their men their lunch-break between twelve and one so that Edith would have an hour of peace before leaving her room. The result of this was that they began again when the dining-room had filled up, and the whole dividing wall vibrated with the machine-gun rattle of the drill plus the voices raised to be heard above it. At least one luncheon party was held against this background. Edith's health deteriorated and the club secretary, worried for her safety, implored me to arrange for a nurse to look after her, at least during the night.

Edith, whose freedom for the greater part of her life had been curtailed by nurses and governesses, would be adamant on the subject, I knew. It was no use asking her permission. I also knew that the alternative might well be another spell in hospital. So I took my courage in both hands, hired the nurse and arranged for her to present herself at the club when I would be there to take the brunt of Edith's anger.

She was angry because she felt betrayed. Yet another trusted associate was beginning to manage her life and to interfere with her liberty. Fortunately she liked the nurse and allowed her a trial period. She began to enjoy the comfort of being looked after, of having someone to talk to in the long hours of the night when *angoisse* threatened. The first hurdle towards proper care had been jumped. With the nurse came better conditions and so better health, and the inner-ear condition was diagnosed and treated. But the noise remained.

At this point Henry Cecil intervened. It so happened that an influential member of the offending firm was a warden at the Putney church to which he belonged. Henry Cecil spoke to him, explaining the situation, and at last positive action was taken.

'I am most deeply grateful to you,' Edith wrote to Barbara Cecil. 'Harry has been most helpful and kind and the noise at present is only like that which might be made by a fleet of giant mice superintending ship-building.'

The respite, alas, was only temporary. Promises to regulate the use of the drill and to finish the work by a certain date were not honoured. I have no doubt that an attempt was made to honour them, but the work had to be completed and the noise continued until it was.

Edith, in much the same spirit no doubt as her Plantagenet ancestors withstood the siege of their castles, refused persuasion, compulsion, bribery, and threats to move out of her room. Two nurses became necessary. As she herself was living on a diet of smoked salmon and champagne—the only sustenance she could be persuaded to take—she insisted that her nurses had the same. Mr Raper was instructed to drive the night nurse home in the hired Daimler. The bills were astronomical.

Meanwhile she amused herself by writing searing letters to her offending neighbours (most of which were, fortunately, given to me to post) and by devising schemes of revenge, which varied from day to day and which had an oddly exotic flavour. One morning, when I rang to see how she was, she informed me that she was ill but feeling very revengeful. 'I am going to occupy myself by buying vipers from the Pets Department at Harrods, nurture them in my room until they are fully grown, and then send them parcel post next door.'

Letters to friends became vehicles for her irritation. Typical of these was one written to me when I was away with a cold; it was focussed on a woman who had annoyed her at a party she gave for the Cecils. She wrote that she 'must have aroused in their minds the conjecture that either I had stolen a figure from Madame Tussauds, or that one of the mummies locked up in a cupboard in a Rhyl lodging house had somehow escaped. She gave no sign of life excepting to scratch (never the most attractive of occupations) and to be fearfully rude to Betsy Whitney.'

After her article on Wyndham Lewis had appeared in the *Observer*, a letter was published in his defence written by T. S. Eliot. She dismissed it as 'priggish' but was more upset by it than she cared to admit. She retaliated by circulating the following note to her friends:

'I've not read Mr Eliot's *Book of Practical Cats*, so can you tell me if it is true that he is the author of these lines?

> I tort I taw a Puddy Tat
> A-creeping up on me.
> You did, you taw a Puddy Tat,
> The Puddy Tat was me!

I wonder what put it into my head that he is the author? . . .'

Then in May, 1961, she had a letter from Paul Hindemith, which led to a visit from the composer and his wife.

Nobody could have looked less like the conventional composer than this genial little gnome of a man with his large, kind wife. The result of their meeting was a suggestion that was to occupy Edith's imagination for years to come. He came to ask her permission to set two of her poems, 'Dirge for a New Sunrise' as a baritone aria with orchestra, and 'Heart and Mind' for men's chorus and orchestra, and to suggest that she should write the libretto for a one-act musical comedy—an opera to be created without the 'usual operatic nonsense', as he put it, written in the spirit of her *English Eccentrics*. Unfortunately for the world, Hindemith died before he could carry out any of his ideas, but Edith felt honoured by his interest and comforted because of it.

In the meantime the conversion was finished and peace reigned once more at 49 Grosvenor Street. But the ordeal had left its mark. The disease of the middle ear had affected her balance so that she was afraid to walk. A wheel-chair was brought into constant use, and her habit of staying in bed grew until it was only when she entertained that she got out of it—and not always then.

Worse than any physical effect, however, was the lowering of her morale. She had been conscious, all her life, of the tragedy of the human situation, but she had been able to answer it by creative activity and by her wit. Now morbid pre-occupations obsessed her. She continued to read the papers each day, but instead of relating to me the scandal that amused her, she would remember only the cases of cruelty, which inflamed her imagination to the exclusion of all else.

For the first time in my knowledge of her she became conscious of mortality as a present possibility. Her resistance being low, she picked up a germ which sent her temperature rocketing, a crisis which was the first in the long battle for survival that lay ahead.

'I am now recovering,' she wrote to Graham Greene, 'but have had rather a grim time, as one of the old girls here endowed me with a serious virus—so bad that I ran a temperature from 103 to 105 every day for nearly a week. Then one day it made a spirited attempt to get to 106, which would have meant "goodbye", and the nurse, also a Catholic, thought she ought to worry them at Farm Street. However, just as she was going to do this, I was restored to 104 and, apart from feeling like death, am recovering.

'During this time I was pestered by reformers. How I hate high-minded people!'

From which account it will be evident that her fighting spirit was far from subdued. A proof of her growing awareness of mortality is the poem, 'A Girl's Song in Winter'. To me one of the loveliest of her later poems, it was written in the midst of the chaos of these months, although, as Stephen Spender asked for it for a special edition of *Encounter*, it was not published until some time later.

I can remember vividly the night she called me in to hear it for the first time. She lay on her bed, her face very white above her woollen cardigan. 'I have written a new poem,' she said, 'and I think it's quite good.' She began to read it to me but could not go on. I took it from her and finished it in silence, and the knowledge of what had made her write it was heavy in us both.

Chapter Twelve

Perhaps it does one good to be angered and distressed by the unfamiliar.
Edith Sitwell to Elizabeth Salter

THE PROBLEM of Edith's health was dealt with, for the time being at least but there remained the more difficult task of putting her mind at rest. Her old enemy the Inland Revenue, with its apparently vindictive habit of demanding large sums of money long after it had been spent, was 'at it again'.

'The London Income Tax people (tireless nuisances that they are),' she wrote to me, 'write to ask if I gave satisfaction in my last situation and the address of the latter and when, if at all, I left.

'I think I shall reply that I was last employed in a menial capacity by Miss Irmegarde A. Potter, of 8, The Grove, Leamington Spa, in 1911 but that I did not give satisfaction. There was some small unpleasantness and I was dismissed without a character.

'I enclose two cheques for the World's Sweethearts,' she wrote to her friend and accountant Robert Covington. 'They seem to think I sleep with my accounts and their letters under my pillow (wearing them, I suppose, about my person in the day-time).

'I don't, and I forget what it is that the creatures want to know now. . . . I have already explained the proportion of living expenses to them once. Do you think if I asked my Professor to translate it into Latin they might get the matter into their heads? . . .

'P.S. I read, last week, that a poor Income Tax gentleman had a fit in a train and that nobody went to help him. I regret this, on humanitarian grounds.'

It was evident that action of some kind would have to be taken. Her pride would not allow her to turn to her family for help, and only the support of Robert Covington and of Charles Musk, a director of Coutts Bank, prevented her financial troubles, rumbling below the surface, from actually erupting. On the advice of trusted friends, she decided to sell her manuscripts, and I judged it the moment to mention the pile of paintings stacked against the wall of her Paris flat. She at once saw the chance of renewing interest in the work of Tchelitchew, and agreed that they too should be sold, deciding to keep only those she valued most. Two such sales, she said, were bound to arouse interest.

The treasure hunt was on.

Locating Edith's collection was rather like peeling an onion: one layer was no sooner removed than another was revealed. It took me two further visits to Paris to gather together all the paintings from her flat. This was partly because she herself had forgotten the number she had bought while she lived there, and partly because the most important of them had been hidden away by Evelyn Wiel during the war. By now she had forgotten where she had hidden them, and it was not until two years later, when she had been forced to vacate the flat owing to illness, that I discovered the last and the best of them all.

The remainder were at Renishaw, as were the bulk of her manuscript books. Once again I set off in my small car and returned with the boot laden with treasure. The visit was a sad one. It was one thing to strip the walls of a shabby, anonymous flat in a foreign country; it was quite another to empty the contents of Edith's bedroom in a home that had been designed and filled with works of art by the family from which she came. I was conscious of desecration. The forbidding façade of this melancholy house, the haughty faces of Edith's ancestors, even the statues shrouded in Sir George's garden, were a mute reproof. It was a grey and dismal day, and in spite of the knowledge that I was acting under Edith's instructions and with the approval of her brother Osbert, I was conscious of an atmosphere of hostility. It did not come from the people I met, from Barbara the sweet-faced house-keeper, from the kindly agent and his family; it emanated from the grey stone walls, from the muffled statues in their weathered canvas hoods, from the discoloured squares on the walls of Edith's room where the paintings had hung. I was glad to escape.

I returned to London with two trunks filled with manuscripts, while the bulk of the pictures was sent down by van. But I had only peeled off the first layer of the onion. More and yet more of these stiff-covered, foolscap-size books, filled with first, second and third drafts of her poems, chapter after chapter of her prose works and sometimes copies of important letters, were to turn up over the years. If ever Edith's sincerity as an artist was in question, these books were proof that she possessed, at least, the infinite capacity for taking pains.

Although she used the same pen for over thirty years, during that time her handwriting changed beyond recognition. Flowing and confident in her later years, it was, in the earlier books, small, neat, almost upright. But in one respect there was no change: she practised her techniques in the first books as she did in the last and as she was to continue to do up to two months before her death.

The world of buying and selling authors' manuscripts was a new one to me and also, I suspect, to Edith. The fact that certain enlightened universities—in the main, transatlantic— were prepared to pay large sums for the privilege of housing the first drafts of a writer's work took the whole matter into the realm of big business. As soon as they heard the rumour of Edith's decision to sell dealers began to get in touch with her. Some were tentative, some were blatant. One flamboyant charlatan, professing to be a private collector, did succeed in obtaining one of the best of her manuscript books. The lure was 'cash on delivery' and I was sternly commanded by him to remain away while the transaction took place. After this experience, I hastened to speed up arrangements with Sotheby's and the dates of the sales were fixed for the end of the year.

In the meantime, as the Sesame Club makes it a rule to close down during the month of August, the problem of Edith's accommodation became more and more urgent. After consultation with her brother Sacheverell and his wife, it was agreed that a flat must be found for her with, if possible, a resident nurse. Neither was going to be easy to find. The flat must have certain definite requirements: it must be near enough for me to be on call; it must be centrally heated, and on one level so that she could move about in her wheel-chair; it must have security of tenure; and it must be small enough to be run with a minimum of staff but large enough to entertain in. A nurse who is willing to manage a household as well as a patient is a rarity. Furthermore, although from now on decisions would be made for Edith in conjunction with her family, there remained the task of persuading her to accept them as they could not be enforced. To the end of her life, there was never any question of action being taken against her wishes.

By the time Edith had agreed to both flat and nurse, I had three weeks in which to find them. Looking back, I can see the reason for her hesitation. Her habit of living had become so fixed that it must have taken courage as well as resignation to agree to so radical and final a change.

Fortunately before she left the club a nurse was recommended, and, within a week of her arrival, an advertisement for a flat appeared in a Hampstead paper that listed the essential requirements. Both were to prove, in the end, a mixed blessing, but at the time they met our urgent needs and were welcomed accordingly. There remained only one major problem: money had to be found for furniture and for the premium. The solution emerged from a conversation I had with Sotheby's, in which I found them prepared to back their judgement and stand by their client. Calling upon her two staunch supporters, Michael Stapleton and 'Mumper' Coates, I began a tour of the shops to inspect curtains, carpets, suites. Because of Edith's horror of germs these could not be second-hand; because of the limited amount at our disposal they could not be expensive. The bits and pieces that remained from her Pembridge Mansions flat—proof indeed that she had known great poverty— were sent down from the room in which they had been stored at Renishaw. Beyond some necessary redecoration builders' fees were out of the question, and so the three of us worked each night, hammering, sewing curtains, making book-shelves. Then one sunlit day in early August the Daimler drew up outside and Mr Raper, her nurse and a wheel-chair bore Edith up in the lift to her new home at 42 Greenhill.

The furnishings were simple but pleasant, sun streamed through the windows, I had put great bowls of flowers throughout the flat. I had, of course, consulted Edith on colour schemes, but she had been content to leave the final decisions to me. Nervously I took her arm and, leaning on her stick, she walked with me down the length of the narrow little hall and pronounced herself well pleased.

I often wonder what were her emotions as she surveyed this, the last but one of her homes, for the first time. After the luxury and elegance of the great houses in which she had been brought up, it must have seemed poky and suburban to a degree. On the other hand it was her own, and she had been without a home of her own for over twenty years. Perhaps too, with her gift for ignoring her surroundings, she was able to remain oblivious of the shell and concentrate on the Tchelitchews that she had kept back from the sales; on the books that were an extension of herself; on the dining-room in which she could still give small luncheon parties; on a sitting-room that was big enough for cocktail parties.

Whatever she felt, her manners were such that nothing but appreciation was shown to me. Her nurse put her to bed in the book-lined bedroom with the specially constructed table on which she could write, and her new life began.

'How happy I am to have got away from the shrieking quarter-wits in my club,' she wrote to Graham Greene. But once again, the fates were against her. Within six weeks I was in hospital, the nurse proved to be unwilling to manage the household, and Edith found herself faced with a problem that had not been hers for many years—the headache of staff trouble.

'My young cook has got engaged to a very nice young man,' she wrote to me in hospital, 'who, unhappily, bears a moustache. His future mother-in-law took a dislike to the moustache, whereupon the household burst into tears. "Oh, Dame Edith," the cook said, "he has such a wonderful bass voice." Between ourselves, my dear, I can't think where he keeps it.'

It was Edith's way of transforming disaster into a good

story. Distressed at my being in a public ward—which she only found out because of a visit she insisted on paying me, in spite of her great difficulty in getting about—she tried to lighten my spirits with amusing stories. When I came out of hospital I found the nurse at daggers drawn with the *cordon bleu* cook engaged for luncheon parties and the housekeeper airing her underwear in the sitting-room. What was far more serious, however, was that Edith was being kept under such deep sedation that, when I rang to congratulate her on the success of her two sales, she neither knew who I was nor comprehended her own good fortune.

My convalescence came to an abrupt end. I rang her doctor, who naturally enough chose to doubt me rather than the nurse; but a surprise visit on his part convinced him. Another consultation was then necessary with her family, and as a result I agreed to undertake the management of her affairs, both personal and public. Fortunately their trust in me made such a decision possible. 'I can never tell you how grateful we are to you for your care and affection for Edith,' Sachie wrote. It was on the strength of the confidence shown in me by both Edith's brothers that I was able to take on a responsibility that was very often to seem too great, complicated as it was by the jealousies and misunderstandings that inevitably surround the famous. These were made worse by Edith's tendency, exaggerated by physical debility, to confide in whoever happened to be near her at the moment, whether nurse, housemaid, a relative, or myself.

'My friend the baby Owl,' she said in her memoirs, 'had to snore in order to attract the attention of mice. Throughout my life, I have been so unfortunate as to attract mice (of the human species) without the effort of snoring.' It was the lure of her confidence which attracted the mice, a confidence born of trust that was too great and judgement that was too haphazard. The most pressing need was to find a nurse who would not only be dedicated to Edith's happiness, but able to sustain this burden of trust. Grappling with the problem, I decided to advertise in such a way as to appeal to the idealists in this exacting and unselfish profession. Although I made no mention of Edith's name, I received over a hundred replies. With Renée Hart, a young devotee of Edith's,

I began the sifting process. We interviewed middle-aged ladies with vague nursing experience and whimsical attitudes, who would have driven Edith into a rapid decline; sturdy matrons with the habit of command, who would have terrorised her; bright young things with social aspirations; well-meaning neurotics who paled at the mention of her name. Out of them all came Sister Farquhar, the dedicated nurse we had been looking for. She was to remain Edith's devoted attendant for the rest of her life.

In the meantime the press had been far from silent. Ever since the Battle of the Noise they had reported her every step: her appeal to the Prime Minister (at one time her publisher) in the despairing last weeks of her campaign; her invitation to the wedding of the Duke of Kent, the fact that she had been unable to attend because she had been made so ill by the 'shattering rumpus', and the poem 'Prothalamium' she had written for the occasion; her move to Hampstead and her decision to sell her manuscripts and her Tchelitchew collection.

This last, as she hoped, aroused general interest, particularly as she made no secret of her reason for selling: her need of money. She was pleased at the publicity given to the paintings, but infuriated at the waste of her time.

'I am being driven nearly demented by the newspapers,' she wrote to me. 'They plague me on the telephone and try to come round here and distort anything I may say. We shall never have any peace until somebody loses his temper with a reporter and strings him up to a lamp post.'

One paper, which she described as 'tireless in boosting rubbish and a sworn foe of those who do not produce it', had, in spite of her constant denials, proclaimed her 'practically a millionaire'. She continued: 'In the photograph of me I am endowed with seven fingers, each finger one and a half inches long and three yards broad, as well as a nose that is tied in a bow behind my back.'

In the main, however, the press was not only sympathetic but admiring. In fact the *grande dame* of English literature was in danger of becoming the sacred cow of Fleet Street. Her name was dragged into every possible context, including the publication of a novel by cab-driver Maurice Levinson.

It is a story worth re-telling. Levinson, born and brought up as an uneducated peasant in Russia, had picked Edith up as a fare one night in 1947. Possessed of the kind of good manners rare in his profession, he had opened the door for her to get out and had commented on the books she was carrying. Edith had been impressed to discover that he had written a book—'Because,' Levinson told her, 'although I've had no encouragement, I have always had a compulsion to write'—and made what was for her the unprecedented suggestion that he send his book to her. She sent him a four-page letter afterwards containing a detailed appreciation of his work and suggestions as to what to do next, followed by a gift of her *Song of the Cold*. Maurice Levinson regarded this letter as one of the great encouragements of his career. They did not meet again, but when Levinson justified her enthusiasm and became a well-known writer, the press unearthed the story from their archives and printed it.

Another event that helped to promote her popular image was the visit of Marjorie Proops of the *Daily Mirror* to Greenhill.

The *Daily Mirror* had ensured Edith's allegiance for life by being the first of the newspapers to publish her poetry, and she remained an assiduous reader of this, as well as of the more erudite newspapers. Her final crusade was a campaign against cruelty to animals, and it was a comment from Miss Proops on this subject that attracted her attention. She wrote to her and in reply the journalist asked for an interview.

As Miss Proops would be the first to agree, theirs was an unlikely combination: the lioness of the literary *salons* was, on the face of it, a dubious subject for 'Marj' of the *Daily Mirror*. That the article was a success can be measured by a rare lack of distortion. A double-page spread portrayed Edith in her large bed with a turban worn above her white velvet bed-jacket, giving such advice as, 'All women should spend a day a week in bed,' and, 'The way to remain young is never to think about oneself and not to worry about such unimportant trifles as whether or not the laundry has come back.' Here was the authentic stamp of the eccentric, but here, too, was the fighter who cared enough about suffering to wage defiant war against it, even when she was so frail that the vitality that emanated from her seemed to come from the overheated air around her bed. And here was the feminine woman of small vanities, asking interestedly about the latest colour in nail-polish, talking about the hats that were still bought for her at Whiteley's, discussing jewels, clothes and manners.

Then, in November of 1961 came the announcement of Edith's forthcoming memoirs.

As I have said, she had no wish to write them, and had it not been for the need to make money, she would never have done so. Written in failing health and vexation of mind, they present a distorted image of an essentially kindly human being. But the writing of them represented the challenge and the stimulus necessary for the creative artist that she remained until her death. If her memoirs needed any justification, this was it.

Her decision to write her memoirs was brought about by a young editor with the gift of persistence, Graham Nicol of Hutchinson. When he first approached me with the suggestion, my answer was discouraging. Arrangements were made for him to come and see her, however, and from then on he visited her once a week until the arduous task was finished. Out of the humiliation of illness, out of the demands from Evelyn Wiel for money that she did not have, out of the memory of the years clouded by Helen Rootham's invalid domination, out of her enforced departure from her family home, came the bitter concept of a life that had been *Taken Care Of*. Her original title had been *More in Sorrow*, which I for one urged her to use, but her publishers preferred the other and so it remained.

Graham Nicol's visits established a routine which was to remain the pattern of her life until the end. She would work in the mornings on a chapter until her strength gave out, and then she would read the papers and write letters. Edith was a letter-writer of the old school, an assiduous correspondent who believed that a letter, like conversation, must amuse. Graham Greene, whose absences from England provided an incentive, received letters during this period which reflect not only her admiration for his work but the bond of their Catholicism. They also provided an outlet for the invective of which she was a mistress.

Rose Macaulay's *Letters*, published at that time, inflamed the accumulated irritation of years. The cause of Edith's dislike of Miss Macaulay I never fathomed, although she did criticise her apparent hypocrisy with regard to money after her will had refuted the popular belief that she was a poverty-stricken writer. There must, however, have been more to it than that. When Edith gave her reading in aid of the restoration of the Stonor chapel, she was told that Miss Macaulay was waiting to congratulate her in the foyer and was reluctantly persuaded to receive her.

'My dear Edith,' Rose Macaulay said fervently, 'I simply had to come.'

'My dear Rose,' Edith answered sweetly, 'I never thought you would make it.'

Now, four years later, she wrote to Graham Greene: 'Alec Guinness and I are in a passion with Saint Rose Macaulay, D.B.E. I always thought her a very nasty trivial insignificant woman and how right I was. Her letters "fair turn me up". She couldn't write and ought never to have been born—if she was. Perhaps like Venus, she simply rose from the foam.'

The death of her beloved little tabby cat, who had been installed during my absence in hospital, caused Edith such distress that I knew a substitute must be found. I returned one day with a cream kitten of such nobility of countenance that Edith christened him 'Leo' and took him to her heart, and not many months later a companion, 'Shadow', an indomitable blue-point Siamese, was procured. So began the reign of the cats at Greenhill.

One day, some months later, I arrived to find a small black kitten with wild green eyes crouched on one corner of Edith's bed. He had turned up at the kitchen door, obviously a stray with a strong instinct for survival. Edith took him in at once and would listen to no arguments as to the impracticability of three cats in one small flat.

'Belaker' had arrived.

Not many months later, yet another perfect, coal-black,

green-eyed stray appeared at the back door. This time
Sister Farquhar put up some real opposition. Four cats in
one flat, none of them able to go outside in the courtyard—
it was too much. I agreed. Edith agreed. The trouble was,
not one of us had the heart to eject him.

'Orion' had come to stay.

Inevitably in the new flat there was a problem of noise.
Edith's nerves could stand no more, but in a mansion block
of flats certain intrusions were unavoidable. I began to dread
the daily telephone call with its account of late-comers
banging the lift door outside her bedroom, or of children
shrieking and yelling under her windows. On this particular
subject Edith had developed an exaggerated personal
grievance. She threatened to get an air-gun to fire above the
heads of the children; she used her charm on the caretaker
to prevent the banging of the lift doors. I found myself
having to ring up total strangers with a request that they
refuse their offspring acccess to a public courtyard; phrases
such as 'I am sure you will appreciate that an old lady in
Dame Edith's state of health' rose automatically to my lips.
The noise crises ebbed and flowed, and with each one it became clearer that sooner or later Edith must have a house of
her own.

In the meantime there was also the problem of the
dailies.

Sister Farquhar, who by now had taken over the management of the flat, preferred daily help to a residential house-
keeper, and our enquiries led us to a nearby school of
students. Nice-looking, well-bred young ladies, anxious to
earn extra pocket money by cleaning for Dame Edith Sitwell,
appeared, only to drop away as soon as the job became less
romantic. One of them had to be prevented from assuming
the role of daughter of the house, and another from handing
round her card at a cocktail party for which her help had
been enlisted.

Middle-aged ladies with no ambitions and no other
attributes than skill with the brush had to be found. Their
task was not an easy one. The use of the Hoover in Edith's
hearing was forbidden, and she viewed the cleaning of her
bedroom as an intrusion on her peace. The most lenient of

employers in other ways, she was irrational on the subject of housework. But her cleaners forgave her, as everybody who looked after her forgave her; and when allowed into her presence they always left with the conviction that they had gained a special place in her affections.

Chapter Thirteen

You need never grow old except in your body.
Edith Sitwell to Marjorie Proops, 1962

THE YEAR 1962, like the year 1959, was for Edith great
and glorious. There was this difference, however: in 1959 it
was Edith who appeared before the world; in 1962 the world
came to her. Reporters, radio men, photographers, television interviewers, made the pilgrimage to Hampstead.
'There is a Greenhill far away,' her friends would quote rue-
fully, after a half-hour of battle with north-bound traffic.
They came to see her just the same. All the daily papers
rang for an interview at one time or another. *Life* magazine
did a special feature, and finally, after her 'Memorial' concert, the B.B.C. featured her as their guest for the 200th
edition of 'This is your life'.

More important to her than anything else, was the publication of three books by Macmillans: *Fanfare for Elizabeth*,
which was re-issued; the best-selling *The Queens and the Hive*;
and her last slim volume of poems, *The Outcasts*.

The year was ushered in quietly enough. Edith, who had
a fervent dislike of festival seasons because they disrupted
such necessary organisations as post offices and printing
presses, preferred to spend Christmas and the New Year
quietly with her nurse and myself. Even so, the act of cele-
bration was for our benefit rather than hers. Christmas Day
had significance for her only in so far as it related to the birth
of Christ. She seldom discussed religion with me, but my
impression was that her conversion was deeply felt, though
unorthodox. She might be described as a 'natural' Catholic.
Through talking to her and reading her works, I came to the

conclusion that her acceptance of the Catholic faith represented not so much a change in outlook as the logical conclusion of a way of thought.

'In Edith Sitwell's poems,' Allanah Harper writes, 'good and evil disappear in the wholeness of the Absolute which is beyond all duality.' This reaching towards an over-all harmony through divergence, the recognition of a pattern recurring in natural phenomena (which brought her into such close sympathy with the work of Lancelot Law Whyte), found its fulfilment in the Catholic faith. An essentially complex nature, she aspired towards simplicity and valued the pure in heart. I noticed that, although she often 'fussed' at the prospect of a visit from her priest, after she had received the Mass a serenity that was by no means integral to her personality evidenced itself. This suggested an acceptance that was far deeper than sometimes appeared to be the case. As I am not a Catholic, I hesitated to question her, but I did once ask her the reason for her conversion. Her answer to me was much the same as her answer to the press, that she sought the 'discipline, the fire and the authority' of the Church. She had been greatly impressed by the simple faith that illumined the faces of the peasants in the church at Montegufoni, and, she added, she considered herself unworthy of it. This humility, which underlay the idiosyncrasies of her personality, seemed to me to be the core of her sincerity as a person, and as a poet. Behind the capricious, witty, dangerously, often mendaciously polite woman, was the 'Sitwell soul' that stood in awe of the ultimate reality and remained uncorrupted before the mystery and the miracle of life.

The longer she spent in bed, the more reading became her favourite occupation, but her frailty made handling books and using her eyes for long periods out of the question. Her old friend Jack Lindsay became a victim of this handicap. As his output was tremendous, and as he was in the habit of sending her a copy of every book, she began to find their accumulated weight intolerable. Politeness compelled her to read and acknowledge the books of her friends, but when she could no longer do so her reaction—as always when forces appeared to conspire against her—was a personal sense of grievance. Jack Lindsay was asked to send no more books, and so ended a friendship which in 1947 she had described as 'one of the most important things in my life'.

The publicity given to her by the newspapers added to the number of 'pests'. She wrote to Jeanne Stonor: 'On an average I get two manuscripts the size of the week's laundry at the Charing Cross Hotel a day—of ghastly verse accompanied by the command to proclaim the writers geniuses and place their masterpieces with publishers. I am nearer to committing murder than I have ever been in my life.'

As an antidote to such murderous impulses and as an alternative to reading, television was installed. Although she had appeared on it often enough, to my knowledge she had never looked at it. It cannot be claimed that she became a television convert. Her reasons for permitting the one-eyed monster were partly that she regarded it as entertainment for her nurses, and partly because her housemaid at the Sesame Club, of whom she had been very fond, had been enthusiastic about Tony Hancock and Edith was anxious to find out if he was really so funny. She found Henry Cecil's television series *Brothers-in-Law* amusing enough to have warranted the experiment, and she wrote to ask Henry Cecil if she might quote a line from one of the episodes, that a certain judge made 'Genghis Khan look like Godfrey Winn'. 'Although,' she remarked to me, 'Godfrey Winn was wonderfully brave during the war.'

Her incapacity also gave her time to indulge in voluminous correspondence. Her letters are further evidence, if any is needed, of the fact that she was, in the strictly executive sense of the word, a writer. In other words, to pick up her pen was an automatic reaction to feeling. Pleased, outraged, irritable, inspired, she wrote her emotion down, working it into a letter to a friend, a poem, a description, a quotation or, very often, into a letter to the papers. When she found a story that pleased her, she memorised it by the arduous method of including it in each letter she wrote; the tendency to be repetitive shows clearly in her correspondence of these years.

Her letters to the papers concentrated on her campaign against cruelty, particularly cruelty to animals. These appeared in many of the popular dailies and answers poured in, adding to her store of unwilling knowledge of pain inflicted on helpless creatures. Whatever good her letters may have done for her campaign, their effect on her was disastrous. Every crank in the country saw in her a sponsor of his cause.

'Because I wrote a letter to the papers saying that a fresh law about cruelty should be passed,' she wrote to Lancelot Law Whyte, 'everybody with a bat in the belfry has released the bats on to me, told me the stories of their lives, described the symptoms of their rheumatism, etc. I don't know who they are or what any of it has do to with me.'

In July, she rang me in a passion of rage. She had just been reading about a poor little fox who, while still alive, was torn to pieces by the hounds. 'And the little pets who allowed this to happen have been acquitted of cruelty.' By the time I came to see her that evening, she had devised a slogan: 'Sport is sport, and I wish I had a pack of man-eating tigers.'

The limitations of her life at this period, as well as the proximity of her four beloved cats, increased her feeling for animals, which had always been strong. From the age of four when she fell in love with a peacock, creatures of every kind had brought warmth into the 'ineffably cold and lonely' childhood that she describes. The cat species remained her favourite, and of these the lion dominated her imagination. Her appreciation was unsophisticated. When her friend and agent Jean LeRoy gave her an early copy of *Born Free*, she bought the book by the dozen to give to her friends. Many of her poetic images were drawn from the lion, as, for instance, these lines from one of her favourite poems, 'Heart and Mind'.

Remember still the flowering of the amber blood and bone,
The rippling of bright muscles like a sea,
Remember the rose-prickles of bright paws . . .

She was as agonised by man's exploitation of animals as the first reformers must have been by the institution of slavery. Like all people whose instincts have not been civilised out of existence, she possessed a strong sense of communication with animals. Her protective sympathy was outraged not only by cases of individual cruelty, but by the greedy exploitation of factory farming and by scientific tortures condoned because of their possible benefit to mankind. She was not a vegetarian, nor did she attempt to rationalise her emotions. She felt and so she acted. She was sometimes anachronistic, as when she recommended the use of stocks as a punishment by ridicule for cruelty, but her campaign was no whimsy of old age. The emotion she brought to it was exaggerated by her general debility, but it was only one campaign in the 'lifetime long running battle'. It was a battle that she did not, because she could not, win, but she left her mark.

In her jottings for her *Poet's Notebook* that she was still hoping to revise, I came across this quotation under the heading of *Animals*:

'Paul Klee wrote: "I love animals. I neither lower myself to their level nor do I raise them to my own. Rather do I sink myself first of all into the whole thing and then place myself on a sort of brotherly level among neighbours— among all my earthly neighbours."'

In August *The Queens and the Hive* made its appearance with a flourish of trumpets and the procession of press, radio and television people began. They brought their photographers with them, but, wherever possible, she insisted that Cecil Beaton's latest photographs be used. He had paid a professional visit to Greenhill and the results had been unusually good. The reason she gave for refusing the press photographers was an unlikely one. 'The last lot of pictures taken of me, 'she said, 'were used as advertisements for sea-sick pills.'

This happened to be true. A Portuguese friend had sent her an advertisement for sea-sickness pills in which her face, blown up to life size and at its most melancholy, had been reproduced in a shade of yellow-green to look all too realistically nauseated. I got on to her lawyer at once, only to discover that nothing could be done about it. Fortunately, the insult was sufficiently bizarre to appeal to Edith's sense of the ridiculous and she began to enjoy the reactions of photographers refused for this reason.

The press was full of Sitwellisms. On the subject of the theatre she remarked, 'The English are the victims of bores and will put up with anything.' To Kenneth Allsop she said, 'I am resigned to the fact that people who don't know me loathe me. Perhaps because I am a woman writing poetry. It must be annoying to a man who wants to write to see this horrid old lady who can.' On the subject of dress: 'Good taste is the worst vice ever invented.'

Just as the lion was for her the symbol of greatness, so she used the mouse for purposes of denigration.

'I don't like mousy poetry,' she told Timothy Green, of *Life* magazine. 'I am not afraid mentally or morally of anyone at all. I always win if I have a fair field. Sometimes I am out for years but I get my way in the end.' On the subject of her poetry she told him: 'I wrote one of my best poems in my bath because my mother couldn't get at me.' Some, she said, she had written especially for her own voice. The poems in *Façade* were 'in a way poems of the machine age'.

Loomis Dean, the *Life* photographer, told her tales of exotic assignments in the Near East where the political situation was explosive. But she said to him, 'I know nothing about politics so I hold my tongue. Nato sounds like nudism to me, and I am not an authority on that. Sometimes I have to watch politicians on television and where they get their faces from I can't think. But, when things are at their worst, I read history like *The Sack of Rome*—then I feel that things have been just as bad in the past.'

After *The Queens and the Hive* she was questioned constantly about her much publicised feeling of affinity with Elizabeth the First.

To Timothy Green she said that she used to think she was Queen Elizabeth. 'I was extremely like her when I was young.' On the television programme 'Tonight', she admitted to a belief that she was the re-incarnation of Elizabeth. But when the producer—out, she explained to me, for 'good television'—brought the subject round to that queen's reputation for virginity, Edith, although prepared to meet most challenges that came her way, avoided that one.

Her combative spirit, though mellowed, was not assuaged.

An American woman columnist had had the temerity not
only to correct her grammar, but to follow the correction with
a patronising 'Really, Edith!' This particular columnist was
syndicated in what must have been hundreds of minor newspapers all over America. Edith's press cutting agency had
managed to unearth each separate 'Really Edith!', so that
her morning post repeated the insult like a record in a
groove.

She pondered her reply:

'I cannot call you geese, because geese saved the Capitol,
and your cackling would awaken nobody. I cannot call you
asses, because Balaam's constant companion saw and recognised an angel. I presume you are members of the vegetable
kingdom and the effervescence of which you are so proud is
simply the rotting of vegetables.'

This became a favourite piece at her cocktail parties, which
she now held about once a fortnight. For them she got out
of bed, was dressed and lifted into her wheel-chair by her
nurse and taken to the commanding corner of her sitting-
room so that I could present each guest as he or she arrived.
No matter what the temperature, she wore a short fur coat
over a satin dress, and her latest hat. A new and rather more
incongruous addition to her attire was a pair of carpet slippers
bought by Sister Farquhar to ensure that her feet were comfortable.

Like this she received the Snows, the Cecils, Charles Musk
of Coutts Bank and his wife, Allanah Harper, who brought
along a newcomer to her circle, Sybille Bedford, Elizabeth
Jenkins, the Spenders, the Day Lewises, Simon Michael
Bessie, her American publisher for the *Memoirs*, and her
cousin Anne Cubitt. With Anne Cubitt came Paul Grey.
Dr Grey, whose Russian birth formed a link with Tchelitchew, was the most enduring of the specialists who transformed Edith's flat into a 'home from home for Harley
Street', as she described it. One after the other, specialists of
every conceivable variety arrived, pontificated and made
way for the next.

The visit of George Cukor resulted from Edith's dedication
to him of *The Queens and the Hive*. He came to thank her for it,
and, as an old friend, was received alone for tea. A kindly,

pleasant-looking man, with the relaxed and benevolent charm that has an unmistakably transatlantic flavour, he had been an especial favourite of Edith's since her visit to Hollywood in connection with his projected film of *Fanfare for Elizabeth*.

In spite of every effort on his part, the film did not transpire, partly, no doubt, because of the difficulty of fitting Edith's concept to the Hollywood mould. She used to enjoy quoting her collaborator on the script: 'This is the scene where you have those Cardinal guys threatening the King with everlasting damnation. And the King says, "That's O.K. by me, boys! Go right ahead. You tell your boss the Pope that I am King of England—and to hell with his everlasting damnation!"'

But the root of the trouble, she told me, was Charles Laughton. As far as Hollywood was concerned, Henry VIII was identified for posterity with this excellent but idiosyncratic actor. There was no escape from him. Her trip, however, was not wasted. With her commission she bought two of her famous aquamarines, labelled from then on 'the wages of sin'. In the meantime, as the producers expected her to 'sit like a beachcomber on the shores of Hollywood with no visible or invisible means of support', she returned to England, leaving George Cukor to work for her cause.

In 1954 he wrote to say that he was coming to England to see her as he had been put into a 'flurry of excitement' by a cable from the Oliviers. Vivien Leigh had written to him that 'I'm in love with Edith's script but, as you know, Larry is now so concentrated on Richard that I doubt if anything else would really interest him at the moment.' In spite of this, Cukor believed that Sir Laurence would be won over. His studio was prepared and anxious to go ahead as soon as the Oliviers consented to appear. Though, in the end, his optimism proved unjustified, Edith had been grateful and had conveyed her thanks by means of her dedication of *The Queens and the Hive*.

George Cukor told Edith he had been so anxious to read the book that he had skipped the introductory pages. 'Imagine my surprise when Noel Coward rang me up to congratulate me on the dedication. I said, "What dedication?" And Noel said, "The book is dedicated to you, George." I looked it up and there it was. I've never felt so honoured in my life.'

In the course of conversation Mr Coward had told him how much he had enjoyed *The Queens* and how much he would have liked to write and tell Edith so, but dared not because of the feud that had existed between them for forty years.

'So, Edith,' George Cukor said, 'I said to Noel, "Why don't you go ahead and write the letter? I'm sure Edith will be pleased to get it."'

Noel Coward did as George Cukor recommended, and Edith sent off an immediate wire in answer:

'Delighted. Friendship never too late. Invite you birthday concert and supper Festival Hall October 9th, 8 p.m.'

Since Coward was about to go into hospital he was unable to accept the invitation, but he wrote asking if he might come and see her when he returned to London.

Edith answered that she had been pleased and touched by his charming letter, which she had answered by telegram as she had been suffering from acute writer's cramp. 'How I wish that unprofessional writers would suffer, sometimes, from this disease,' she added.

'The 9th should be a day for all present to remember. Never before, I think, has anyone attended their own Memorial Service. (The press is madly excited at my being 75 and is looking forward avidly to my funeral.)

'I do hope you will find time to come and have a sherry or a cocktail with me when you come to London. Do please ring me up.'

In November Noel Coward took up the offer, choosing tea-time. While we were waiting for his arrival she told me the history of the feud between them.

Noel Coward, when a young man of twenty-three had been invited by Osbert to the performance of *Façade* at the Aeolian Hall. As he admits himself, he did not 'get it', and being as gifted and witty a lampoonist as the Sitwells, he wrote a revue parody, featuring 'Hernia Whittlebot' with grapes in her hair. The joke was on the words—particularly 'Jane,

Jane, tall as a crane'—rather than about Edith herself. But the mischief-makers were at work. One of those dear friends who feel impelled to 'tell one things for one's own good' informed Edith that there was an obvious and infamous implication behind the sketch. Edith retired to bed, suffering from mortification that developed into jaundice, and did not get up again for six weeks. Her brothers made their displeasure felt, and their reaction seemed to Mr Coward, who remained ignorant of the real cause of it, to be so pompous that he carried the joke one step further and expanded his parody into a book of verse. After this, of course, he was delegated to the ranks of the enemy, and things remained in this state until he found himself in New York with Osbert, at a party to which they had been invited as the English guests of honour. Mr Coward's first impulse had been to refuse the invitation, his second to accept and to confront Sir Osbert with the suggestion that he be now forgiven. Sir Osbert's reply was that the hand of friendship could not be extended until he had apologised to his sister. Edith being then in England, Mr Coward did the only thing possible, which was to send off a telegram. Edith's acknowledgement was a cabled statement that she accepted his apology. Though hardly enthusiastic, it did at least indicate that battle stations were closed.

Both Edith and I waited for his ring at the door with some trepidation; Edith because she was to receive a man whom she had regarded as her enemy for forty years; I because I had admired Mr Coward since I had first discovered his work at the age of seventeen. Mr Coward admitted later that he also felt some trepidation. Because of the feud, neither of them had had the slightest idea of what to expect of the other. Their reaction was one of astonishment as well as delight.

They sat opposite each other in Edith's small sitting-room, Mr Coward wearing dark glasses because of a complaint that he described, cheerfully, as 'pink-eye', Edith in her latest hat, her inevitable fur coat and slippers. Mr Coward sipped his tea and refused sandwiches. Edith went through the motions of lifting her cup to her lips and put it down again untouched. I ate the sandwiches, drank my tea and listened.

Mr Coward set the ball rolling by apologising for having hurt her feelings, pleading youth. Edith accepted his apology with a warmth that proved past resentments had not only been banished but forgotten. They then went on to discuss 'Willie' Maugham and his legal battle with his daughter. Although they were on different sides in the controversy— Mr Coward explaining that he had been very fond of Willie's wife and considered her to have been badly treated, and Edith confessing to a dislike of the lady—she admitted having found Somerset Maugham something of a strain. In fact, she had once tried to avoid meeting him at Bumpus by picking up an imaginary book under a table.

'Poor Willie,' she said, 'he simply followed me under the table so that we encountered each other on all fours. "E-e-edith," he said to me, "wh-what are you doing down here?"'

But it was the discovery of a shared enemy that brought them into triumphant accord. Edith, still full of her grievance against the American lady columnist with the syndicated newspapers, found that Mr Coward knew her personally.

'Do tell me,' Edith asked him, 'what is she like?'

Mr Coward's reply was instantaneous. 'My dear Dame Edith, she is one brisk stampede from nose to navel.'

By the time he left they were both regretting the wasted years. As I helped Mr Coward into his coat I told him that I felt I had been present at an historic occasion.

Mr Coward did not indulge in false modesty. 'You have been,' he agreed genially.

It was by no means the end of their acquaintance. Mr Coward sent Edith a painting and his *Collected Short Stories* and Edith sent him the new edition of her *Shakespeare Notebook*, accompanied by a letter.

November 23rd, 1962.

Dear Mr Coward,

I cannot tell you what real pleasure it gave me to see you the other day. I enjoyed our talk so much. Please don't forget you have promised to come and see me again after you return on the 6th. Do ring me up any time and say you are coming.

It was so good of you to send me your *Collected Short Stories*. There are no short stories written in England in our time that I admire more. I think 'Aunt Tittie', for instance, a real masterpiece. I am not a cry-baby, but it brings tears to my eyes every time I read it—and I have read it over and over again. I can't think what you must have gone through, piercing into the hearts of those two forlorn human beings. The end of the story is almost unbearable, you have done more, so quietly, than most writers do by yelling at the tops of their voices.

All the stories have that extraordinary quality of reality, so that, although the endings are perfect endings, one feels the people go on living after the stories, *qua* stories, are finished, and one wants to know what happened to them, beyond the stories.

I am about half way through the book, and shall write again when I am the whole way through it.

I may say that I had a very bad nightmare last night about 'What Mad Pursuit'. I dreamt that George [Cukor] said I had to go and stay with some people in Hollywood for a rest. But I was saved in the end, because the maid had hidden all my belongings, so I missed the boat train by two minutes!

I am having rather a harassing time with lunatics, because I was televised the other day. One wrote to say I ought to be ashamed of myself, and that I have senile decay and softening of the brain—which, oddly enough, made him respect me. Another has written a very long letter about Einstein, telling me I will never get into Space or Time.

I am sending you my *Notebook* on Shakespeare. The cover is so unspeakably appalling that I nearly faint when I contemplate it. I do not know if it is meant as a portrait of me if I turn blue, or if it is supposed to represent a map.

I am not supposed to show any of my autobiography to anyone at all, but I *can't* resist sending you my portrait of Wyndham Lewis, hoping it will make you laugh. I am afraid it is rather a battered copy, but it is the only type-script I have got. Don't bother to return it.

Please do come and see me again very soon.

All best wishes, yours ever,

Edith Sitwell.

P.S. The American monsters who published my *Notebook*, not content with inflicting that scarifying cover on me, won't allow me to be an Hon. D.Litt. of Oxford. One shouldn't mind, but I do take it hard!

Chapter Fourteen

*On very rare occasions and when the stature of
a great artist is at stake,* The Times *is not afraid to eat its words.*
Apology to Edith Sitwell by *The Times*, 1962

It was not for nothing that Edith christened the concert in the Royal Festival Hall in October of 1962 her 'Memorial Service'. The programme, the performers, the list of guests at the supper party afterwards, represented the framework of her life's achievements. Her sense of occasion empowered her to rise to this, the last great public challenge she was to meet. Although she was to dismiss it after the event as 'rather like something macabre out of Proust', she recognised it as the final parading of her colours after a lifetime of battle for recognition. After it, she knew, must come anti-climax. Fighter she remained, but instinct warned her that the last round had been fought and that ahead of her was only the waiting, the resignation and the end.

She did what she always did when faced with an uncomfortable emotion: she turned it into a joke. By calling it her 'Memorial Service', she removed the sting. She began to look forward to it. As she herself was to recite some of her later poems, she went into training with a determination that would have done credit to an Olympic champion. She agreed to a daily treatment by her physiotherapist, although she would sometimes ring me up afterwards in tears because the 'massacre' had been so painful, and to sit for an hour on the edge of her bed and swing her legs. What was more important, she began to accept more nourishment, allowing Sister Farquhar to substitute a cup of despised milk or tea for her favourite mid-morning martini and eating her food with an almost normal appetite. Ironically enough, it was her vanity that told against her health during these last years. She liked to be pale and she liked the flesh to be drawn tightly across her bones. Any suggestion of heaviness in wrists, hands or face horrified her, and she was never more put out than when I inadvertently told her how well she looked because of the colour in her cheeks. Fortunately she was also proud of her voice and she knew that, if she was to be heard in the Festival Hall, it must be stronger. Certainly the perfection of diction which had made it such an exquisite instrument for the language was now impaired. Whether or not she had suffered a slight stroke during the period of my convalescence, as some of her medical advisers thought, or whether it was the effect of a constantly supine position in bed I do not know, but the limpid, vibrant tones were slower and distinctly muffled. At times her tongue seemed to be caught by a word so that it emerged with a slight distortion. She was aware of this and nervous of it. She practised reading aloud, but the effects were not reassuring. Often when I came in to see her she would tell me that she would never be able to recite again. Irene Worth, who was to be one of the two readers of *Façade*, was sent a typescript of her poems in case she decided that she could not, after all, read them herself.

In the meantime, the concert was preceded by an onslaught of dressmakers, hat-makers, manicurists and beauty parlour experts. For her dress she decided on a red velvet, as that had been the material chosen for her by Tchelitchew when she had given a recital in Paris more than thirty years ago. It had long satin sleeves of the same colour and a high, round neck in order to show off the gold collar that she always wore on state occasions. Her hat, modelled on a becoming black straw with a wide, turned-back brim that she already possessed, was gold. Gold, too, were the shoes that were visible in her wheel-chair, below the folds of her skirt. I undertook the polishing of the four aquamarines by the method recommended by her jewellers, Cameo Corner, and the manicurist, who came once a week, gave her a wax treatment for her hands. An appointment was made for a 'facial' to be given by an expert a few hours before her appearance. In spite of her illness and her secluded life, when she was to appear in public she still had her face made up with an attention to detail that would have done justice to a film star, choosing green as the colour of eye-shadow that most effectively accentuated the hooded depth of her eyes. Her lipstick matched the red of her nails. Proud of the fact that it was she who had set the fashion for gold and silver nail-polish in the 1920s, she sometimes experimented by gilding her nails, but for the concert she decided on red as the colour that, at this stage of her life, showed off her hands to the best advantage.

Visitors began to pour in, some of them having travelled especially for the event, like the novelist Carson McCullers. Miss McCullers, in fact, in spite of a recent serious illness, had accepted a lecture engagement in England so that she could also be present at the concert, and rang well in advance to arrange a visit to Greenhill.

Edith had given me her favourite of Carson McCullers' novels, *The Heart is a Lonely Hunter*, which, she said, showed an insight into the world of the adolescent that made her unique. About Carson herself she had a fund of stories, told with affection and exaggeration, from which I had built up a picture very different from Miss McCullers as she appeared that day. Very pale, wearing a fur coat and carpet slippers, she managed the walk down Edith's corridor with the help of a stick and the young nurse in attendance. Slim, younger-looking than I had expected, she managed, in spite of the paralysed arm and the injured face muscles that could sustain a smile for a few seconds only, to convey the atmosphere of the perennial adolescent. Her attitude towards Edith was demonstrative, her southern drawl irresistibly reminiscent of dialogue written by her friend Tennessee Williams.

The effort required for her visit must have been great, and she left as soon as the meal was over. After the concert, when Edith was being driven away in state in the 'Motor', she caught a glimpse of Carson perched forlornly on a seat outside the Hall, waiting for a taxi, and stopped the car to dispatch one of the young men in her entourage to make sure that she was all right.

Any illness of her friends had become almost unendurable to Edith. At her best she had always been nervous of other people's complaints, but now that her own vitality was at so low an ebb, she was depressed beyond measure by them. As a result, her sympathy was overlaid by an irritation that she found difficult to conceal. It was as though her own battle for survival had left her without resources. Her weapon against the intrusion of suffering was anger, and she used it as an antidote to depression.

Shortly before the event, Irene Worth and Sebastian Shaw came to rehearse their reading of *Façade*. It was a gesture of politeness on their part which proved to be of little value, as Edith would have considered it beyond the limits of good manners to have corrected two such artists, whether or not their interpretation differed from hers. What impressed her was their professionalism. Miss Worth, particularly, revealed herself to be a dedicated actress who used her considerable intellect in interpreting a rôle.

Their conversation moved almost at once to the subject of *King Lear*, the new production of which was about to appear in London, and in which Miss Worth was playing Goneril. Edith listened to her ideas with interest. She reguarded *Lear* as the greatest play in the language, quoting the dialogue between Lear and Cordelia, to her of the utmost significance to the play:

LEAR	Speak.
CORDELIA	Nothing, my lord.
LEAR	Nothing?
CORDELIA	Nothing.
LEAR	Nothing will come of nothing: speak again.

Behind this 'huddle of meaningless words,' as Edith described them, lay the answer of the play: that 'Man is nothing'.

By the afternoon of the performance, news came that the concert, organised by those two energetic young men, Francis Sitwell and John Woolf, was booked out. Edith had announced herself able to read, so I left her preparing for her 'facial' and her robing, and arranged to meet her in her dressing-room at the Royal Festival Hall a half-hour before the performance.

By the time I arrived the press were everywhere, their

photographers in readiness for the supper party afterwards, their notebooks ready to catch an incident or a comment for which they knew they would find international coverage. The buzz of anticipation rebounded off the acoustic walls of the Festival Hall. Then the lights were dimmed.

A spotlight caught the scarlet figure in the wheel-chair, turned to face the audience. Behind her Francis Sitwell stood in attendance. Edith rustled her typescript and adjusted her glasses. The business-like way she put on these utilitarian objects created its own contrast. It was as though the intellectual was bidding us forget the illusion created by the great eccentric. 'The effect has been achieved, now we must concentrate on the matter in hand,' she seemed to be saying, while the glasses, perched insecurely on the elegant nose, pushed up the brim of her hat.

I am quite sure that I was feeling more nervous than Edith, as she gave a little upward movement of her free hand to answer the roar of applause. To feel the full impact of the moment when she began to read, one would have had to see it, as I did, against the background of the months that had preceded it; to recall the figure, white-faced and supine, sometimes in tears of fatigue because every movement was an effort, the fragile bone protruding from the flannel nightdress, and the transparent, delicate skin that had remained as vulnerable as it must have been in childhood.

Her voice was deeper, more slurred, rather softer than of old, but on this night there was nobody to say they could not hear. The audience brimmed over with her friends, and from the sea of faces beneath us I saw her former chambermaid Hannah, seated proudly beside Mr Raper in the seats she had given them.

The silence in the auditorium conveyed much more than just the quality of listening. It was the hush of respect. The grand old lady who made a throne out of her wheel-chair and intoned her opulent images was crowned that night by her achievements. She read the poem born of the quotation from St Agnes she had once sent me, 'His Blood Colours my Cheek', the tiny lyric that was the fruit of her sufferings over the Battle of the Noise, 'A Girl's Song in Winter', 'Choric Song' and 'Prothalamium', her last poem, written for the marriage of the young Duke and Duchess of Kent. All but two of the poems had been written since her seventieth birthday.

I was conscious of relief when she was wheeled off the platform. Sister Farquhar was waiting in the wings to shepherd her to the Royal Box, in which she was given pride of place between her brothers Osbert and Sacheverell, winged by their family. With them were Sister Farquhar and myself. As she took her position, Peter Pears was on stage ready to sing Benjamin Britten's arrangement of her 'Still Falls the Rain'. The canticle was followed by a Rossini sonata and a Mozart divertimento and, after the interval, came *Façade*.

Watching Sir William Walton conducting the English Chamber Orchestra, this time with no screen and the two soloists well in evidence, I had a mental picture of 'Miss Sitwell with her Sengerphone' seated behind the controversial screen when *Façade* was first privately performed in the home of Mrs Robert Mathias, with Diana Mathias, then a little girl, holding the Sengerphone, and Diaghilev in the audience, gathering ideas for the ballet he was to plan from it. Edith, overcome by nerves, sank back near to fainting after she had read. I remembered the 'hideous rumpus' that had followed its reception in the Aeolian Hall, when she had been 'nearly lynched' by the inevitable old woman, symbol of the enemy, who had waited, umbrella raised, to smite her. I thought of the last time I had heard Edith herself perform it, before the cheering undergraduate audience at Oxford. I listened to the effervescent bubble of words that took colour from and dissolved into Sir William's witty music, and marvelled at the initial concept that had dared the critics and triumphed over them; at the lifetime of effort that had led to this moment.

As audience to her own work for, as far as I know, the first time in her life, inevitably Edith did not entirely approve of the performance that night. But the critic who was later to quote her words on the subject should have remembered that it was the performer and not the creator of *Façade* who criticised it. As performer, she had a possessive prejudice towards a rôle that she regarded as her own. As creator, she was aware of the tribute being paid to her and responded, joining in the tumultuous applause that followed.

The speakers came back to take their applause. They returned with Sir William, and the applause continued. We waited for the moment when the performers would turn towards the Royal Box, but before this could happen the audience decided to pay its own tribute. The entire three thousand wheeled round to face her. Looking down, the movement of upraised hands was like a current in the sea that swirled in her direction. They clapped, they cheered, they stamped. Edith made an effort to rise out of her wheelchair in acknowledgement but could not. Instead she lifted her hands and waved back, crying without self-consciousness.

Of all the rapturous press reports, her favourite was a piece from the *Daily Sketch*. She rang me next morning in order to read it to me.

'My dear, you must listen to this. Some nice young man that I never met was evidently holding my hand as I went off to sleep. This is what he says about me: "A wonderful, exasperating, intelligent woman, before she pulled up the sheets and slipped into sleep, she said, 'Be kind to me. Like the poet Yeats said, *I have spread my dreams under your feet. Tread softly because you tread on my dreams.*' " According to him, I uttered these famous last words: "Don't trample on me because so many people do." '

' "And then our greatest woman poet fell asleep." Goodness!'

The second of her two 'memorials' that year could scarcely compete with the first. When the suggestion reached me that the B.B.C should make her the subject for their 200th edition of 'This Is Your Life', I knew that she must be warned and, together with her agents and her doctor, hoped that she would refuse it.

Although, in those days, the subject of this programme was kept in total ignorance of the confrontations planned so that they would come as a surprise, in her case this could have proved fatal. A heart murmur that she had apparently had for the greater part of her life had now been diagnosed, and a shock coming so soon after the excitement of the concert might have been too much for her.

As I have already said, it was the knowledge that her coloured maid, Velma Le Roy, had agreed to appear on the programme that decided her. She refused to disappoint her, and so 'This Is Your Life' on Monday 22nd October, 1962, featured, in the words of Eamonn Andrews, 'Dame Edith Sitwell, poet, writer, descendant of Robert the Bruce, the Red Rose Plantagenets and Macbeth'.

A press note after the event pointed out that, although Edith may well have justified the programme, it scarcely did justice to her. Certainly her comments to me when she talked about it later were dismissive. 'It simply did not happen like that,' she complained, and in relation to one of the 'guests' who appeared out of her past, 'Why they dragged that unfortunate man along I cannot imagine.'

However, the research department of the B.B.C had done its best. Her cousin Veronica Gilliat was there to recount the story of the girl who had turned her back on the races on her twenty-first birthday, and she added another eccentricity to those already accumulated by Sir Osbert on the subject of his father by producing the present he had given her on her twelfth birthday—a tortoiseshell cigarette case and holder. Sacheverell filled in the picture of Edith's youth by describing the assiduous girl who filled her notebook with quotations and who had been from the start 'determined to be remarkable'. Her old friend Dr Arthur Waley described the 'strong tea and sticky buns' served at Pembridge Mansions in the early days of her emancipation, which had attracted the best of the young talent in London. He also stressed her aversion to country walks, or, in fact, walking of any kind, except for one walk that they had taken together when they had received their honorary degrees from Oxford University. Even then, he said, Edith had made a fearful fuss about it. Geoffrey Gorer described her love of music halls and her delight when mistaken on one occasion for Nellie Wallace. Diana Mathias, now Baroness de Bosmolet, together with Anthony Bernard, gave first-hand accounts of the cat-calls and pandemonium that greeted the first public performance of *Façade*. Cecil Beaton, who had always thought her 'much better than a model', took the narrative to the days when she posed for his early experiments in photography, enduring long periods on her knees, with her head in a huge Victorian glass dome and her joints cracking loudly in protest. George Cukor and Velma Le Roy represented the Hollywood saga and Marjorie Proops paid her tribute from the first paper to publish her work.

As snapshots from the album of her life, these were representative; as tributes to her stature as a person and as a poet they were scarcely adequate. However, Velma Le Roy's fervent assurance that she was 'the world's most marvellous woman' touched Edith and justified the programme in her eyes. She enjoyed, too, showing her histrionic talents by feigning the enormous surprise she felt was expected of her. On the whole the evening did her no harm; in fact, it lessened the inevitable sense of anti-climax that followed her birthday.

For Christmas of that year I paid my own tribute with a party in her honour at my new flat in Fitzjohn's Avenue. It was the last of her outings for many months. A few weeks later, her lungs began to give trouble and a virus illness threatened to turn into pneumonia. Sister Farquhar broke the news to me that, if she was to survive the winter, she must be got out of London, and preferably out of England. A visit to a warmer climate was mooted. In the end, it was Edith herself who suggested the world voyage, and it happened in this way.

As she, and all of us, had expected, reaction to the festivities of the year before was severe, and to keep her from the depression of anti-climax became my daily occupation. Each morning when she spoke to me on the telephone, and every afternoon on my way to see her, I would rack my brains for a story or a book or some incident that would amuse her. Our conversations round her bed became a daily reassurance, which usually fell on deaf ears. The glory, the excitement, the realisation of acclaim, had given way to a depression to which, Dr Grey said, she had been periodically subject all her life. Sometimes when I went to her room I felt that the Edith I knew was not there. Her speech would be muzzy, her eyes owlish. At other times her mental energy would reassert itself, acting as the dynamo that consumed her scanty fuel, so that her body remained frail and devitalised.

Knowing that the subject of jewels and jewellery was one that was guaranteed to interest her, I told her one day about my last visit to Colombo, when I was taken to a jeweller's shop in the arcades of that mysterious city and shown a ruby the size of my thumb emitting a fire that filled me with the urge to possess it.

Edith turned to Sister Farquhar and then to me.

'Why don't we go?' she suggested.

Sister was delighted at the prospect of escape from the dangerous London air. My own feelings were mixed, as I happened to be in the final stages of a book. But Edith's health had to come first. I went in next day to discuss further plans.

These grew like Jack's beanstalk. Edith, having made up her mind to go as far as Ceylon, decided that she would return via America in order to see her friends *en route*. Although I knew that a voyage held no terrors for her as she was an excellent sailor, I also knew the difference between five days on the Atlantic and ten weeks crossing to the other side of the world and back. Worried about the responsibility of accompanying her, I consulted her doctors and was reassured that, with medical advice obtainable on board, there was no need for concern. Another consolation was that her brother Sacheverell and his wife Georgia were to accompany us as far as Gibraltar. I went to the shipping agent and made the necessary arrangements.

A snag presented itself almost at once. The southbound ships at this time of the year were comparatively empty, but ships across the Pacific were full. To postpone the trip would defeat the object of the voyage—to get Edith out of England as soon as possible. An alternative was suggested. We could change ships in Australia and return on the Dutch vessel, the *Willem Ruys*. This would mean a delay of nearly two weeks in Australia, but the ship would call in at Miami on the way back to England. It looked like the ideal compromise and Edith agreed at once.

I wired for our accommodation in a quiet hotel in Sydney and only when it was confirmed did I allow myself to look forward to our trip. After eleven years of absence I was to have eleven days in Australia. I would see my old friends again and be able to introduce my family to Edith.

If I had any prophetic pangs of drama and disaster, I stifled them with this thought.

Chapter Fifteen

*How many of my readers, I wonder, have also escaped narrowly
from the very jaws of death, because of the myth that holidays are enjoyable?*
Edith Sitwell in the *Daily Mail*, 1927

'I HAVE BEEN very gravely ill—somebody came (uninvited) and gave me that mystery virus that is puzzling all the doctors. I was very ill with that—and then it started turning to pneumonia, with which I was so ill that the doctors have ordered me to go on a sea voyage. I start on Tuesday the 5th March with my nurse and my secretary, heading for the Pacific (the sharks can't be much worse than they are here, sucking one's blood all the time). I return, if intact, in the middle of May.'

So Edith wrote about her forthcoming trip to her friend Lance Whyte. It was hardly an enthusiastic announcement, but by this time her deep-rooted dislike of holidays had set in. More than once she had expressed herself on the subject, particularly when a friend, returned from abroad, regaled her with his or her experiences. One of her favourite articles of those she wrote for the *Daily Mail* begins: 'If Judgement Day arrived and the secrets of men's hearts were discovered, those hearts would confess their sins without a qualm. But one hypocrisy they would cling to. They would insist on the fact that they had enjoyed their holidays, no matter how frightful the experience would have been.'

To guard against the 'holiday atmosphere' she filled one trunk with books and another with manuscripts, together with two large bottles of ink.

Her main dread was of the ambulance journey to the ship. Our instructions were to be on board by one o'clock, which meant that we had to drive to Tilbury through the worst of the morning traffic. Edith, travelling at ambulance speed, allowed three hours for the journey. Mr Raper and I, bringing the luggage in the Daimler, gave her a half-hour start. As a result she arrived before we did. and I left Mr Raper, looking as indomitably ruddy as ever, under the sullen March skies, while I went to make sure she was all right. I found her already ensconced in her cabin, entertaining the ship's assistant purser with the story of her arrival.

'Oh, my dear, Sister and I have just had the most fearful experience,' she greeted me. 'My wheel-chair was seized by two old gentlemen, who looked as if they were covered in seaweed and were retainers of Neptune. I was absolutely terrified. We were half-way up the gangway and they got my right ankle caught in my wheel-chair and almost broke it. I yelled, and poor Sister had to do battle with them before they would release it, which was rather difficult as they had got it impacted. It's my belief that they were too deaf to hear a word either of us said. It was like a kind of torture in the Tower in the time of Elizabeth.'

When Edith reached the stage of transforming a crisis into a good story, it was a sure sign that it was over. I went back to organise the luggage on board and to cope with the press, assisted by Francis Sitwell who had come to see us off. When I got back I learnt that although we had booked A-class cabins, the *Arcadia* had given Edith a luxury stateroom. It was the first of many acts of generosity from this courteous and friendly ship and was especially appreciated when the first of the rough weather that was to dog us on this health voyage of Edith's hit us.

After a few hours of battle in which I turned the colour of the Portuguese advertisement, I gave in and retired to my bunk, but Edith survived the first of her ordeals without discomfort. To Jeanne Stonor she wrote, 'Elizabeth was fearfully ill. I am a very good sailor and wasn't.' In the throes of the death-wish that assailed me, I remembered to be thankful for this.

At Gibraltar we said goodbye to Sacheverell and Georgia and next day, in the full blaze of the Mediterranean sun, Edith gave a party in her cabin for the Captain, the Staff Captain and the hostess.

Ships' captains, whose authority in their own domain is absolute, have an aura that separates them from ordinary mortals on board. They are the Crown, the Church, the Law. No ship's captain, however, can ever have been less authoritarian or less pompous than Captain Mayne. Slight, friendly, with an enquiring rather than a commanding manner, he proved to be as intelligent as he was kind. Two or three times a week, he called in to Edith's cabin for drinks before lunch, to talk books with her.

The Mediterranean settled into its indigo calm. Edith settled down to her memoirs. During those first peaceful weeks she wrote the early chapters. Although she had started work in London, it was on board ship, lying in her stateroom with her windows firmly closed against the sea breezes that she had been ordered to breathe, that she polished and completed the brilliant introduction to the book.

Our routine was as fixed as at Greenhill. Sister, who had an adjoining cabin, attended to most of Edith's needs, staunchly refusing relief from the ship's nurses either in or out of port because, she said to me, 'I have seen as much of the world as I want to see'. I called in each morning to help Edith with her entertaining and each afternoon, at the usual hour, to discuss the progress of her book and to amuse her with stories about our fellow passengers. These she resolutely refused to meet except in cases which touched her imagination or her sympathy—as, for instance, a woman who had lived through a plane crash, and a banker who remained permanently intoxicated because he was dying of cancer of the throat.

Crises inevitably arose. I came in one evening to find her looking tragic because, she said, 'the nib of my fountain pen is giving way and won't form letters. So useful in mid-ocean.' A substitute was found which she accepted with reluctance. Her thirty-year-old pen, given to her by her brother Osbert, had become a part of her.

'To write poetry,' she explained, 'I have to feel what I am writing with my fingers.'

However, as she was engaged on what was to her the poor relation of her craft, the writing of prose, she accepted the substitute as a temporary measure.

As we approached the tropics and I came in to see her

with Coleridge's lines sounding in my ears, as always in those hot, windless latitudes—'Day after day, day after day, we stuck, nor breath nor motion; as idle as a painted ship upon a painted ocean'—I found her near to tears of indignation because Sister would leave the windows open to let in 'those damned sea breezes'. She had been in a draught all day, she said. I tried to point out the good that it was doing her, but my soothing words had no effect. Shortly afterwards the windows were closed again and peace was restored.

She worked on one bed and used the adjoining one as a depository for her books and manuscripts. When I came in she would usually read aloud to me, especially if she was pleased with what she had written. I made the interesting discovery that she was drawing from autobiographical notes that she had made from time to time throughout her life, and I regretted again that she had not been persuaded to write the book years before. If she had, it might have emerged as a masterpiece of its kind, as the manuscripts now stored in Texas University bear witness.

The tropics traversed, and the ceremony of 'Crossing the Line' blessedly behind us, we sailed at last into Colombo harbour.

It was a hot March morning and the water, steel-grey and greasily calm, was alive with fishing boats, steamers and Singhalese boys fishing for pennies. Knowing that our call at Colombo represented that part of the trip for which I was uniquely responsible, I felt somewhat nervous. I had written to the High Commissioner and to a private jeweller with the exotic name of Abdul Ameer. It was Mr Ameer's representative who boarded the ship to greet us and who offered himself at once as my guide.

There was no question of Edith being able to go ashore herself, and the best I could do was to bring back a hoard of treasure from which she could select the jewel that she intended to buy. My guide and I sallied forth, crossed the crowded little bay in a small and smelly ferry-boat and arrived at the shop of Mr Abdul Ameer. It was plain from the start that the jewels I had seen in 1949 were things of the past. Their counterparts might still exist, but not at the same prices. Mr Ameer, a handsome, grey-headed Singhalese, with dark, evasive eyes, showed me his collection, and with a showman's sense of drama left his *pièce de resistance* to the last. It was a large and shimmering aquamarine, pale but beautifully cut. To my surprise, though perfectly agreeable to my taking his collection to the ship, he chose not to accompany me; so gathering up my bagful of topazes, amethysts, sapphires, zircons and aquamarines, worth several thousands of pounds in all, I set off once more. Something in his manner made me faintly uneasy, but I put it down to a natural reluctance to allow such treasure to leave his shop in the hands of a stranger. His guide escorted me to the docks and left me to take the ferry back alone. He would meet me there at two-thirty and we would return together for the bargaining process that would complete the deal.

Edith spent the lunch hour in selecting the jewel of her choice. Inevitably it was the largest of the aquamarines, and I knew that I must become a tougher bargainer than I was by nature. Before I went down for my meal I was summoned for drinks by the purser.

'How did you manage about the jewels?' he enquired casually.

I told him.

'Did the guide come with you back to the ship?'

I answered in the negative and he looked grave. 'He knows as well as I do that it's illegal to leave the shore with unbought jewels. If they had caught you they would have assumed that you were smuggling them and arrested you on the spot. What's more,' he added, 'no white woman's name would be powerful enough to have got you out of jail.'

I kept this interesting piece of knowledge from Edith and returned with the jewels burning a hole in my handbag. I was not arrested. The bargaining session resulted in no less than one hundred pounds being knocked off the price, and I returned to the ship well satisfied. I admit, however, that before I slept that night a vision of a hot and sticky Singhalese jail floated into my consciousness.

At Fremantle, our next port, Edith was not left in peace. The Australian reporters refused to accept without a struggle the fact that she had made a journey to their land merely for the sake of the voyage, and when we docked at five-thirty in the morning, the press were on board waiting for her. Two starry-eyed ladies from the Society of Women Writers brought a bouquet and a poem in her honour. Edith's politeness made captives of them all, and headlines appeared in every capital city in the country that 'Dame Edith likes Australians' and 'Dame Edith thinks that the vitality of the arts will come from Australia'.

The press thronged her cabin at Adelaide and Melbourne. 'The Woman who Lives up to her Legend' appeared as a feature in the *Adelaide Advertiser*, and 'Poetess with an Air of Command' took up two columns of the *Melbourne Age*.

She did, however, refuse to be photographed. 'If I had two faces you could have one,' she told them. Instead she gave them her hands, and the *Melbourne Age* featured them, laden with aquamarines, to accompany their description of the poetess as 'detached from the earth as a recumbent marble figure in an English cathedral'. She complimented them on their consideration, telling them that in England poets were persecuted. 'I've been burned as a witch every year since I was twenty-seven,' she told them.

By the time she reached Sydney Edith was exhausted. The early arrivals in port, the constant interviews, had proved too much of a strain. I put off the press with the promise of a conference before our departure; then, waiting until the rest of the passengers had disembarked, we smuggled her off the ship to her hotel.

Fortunately on that sunlit morning of our arrival, Sydney lived up to its reputation. The magnificent, untidy sprawl of streets bejewelled by the harbour alive with craft and spanned by a bridge of grace and grandeur, took Edith by surprise. The gardens, blazing with flowers and bushes of exotic foliage, pleased her. The room she had been given was large, panelled in wood and filled with light. The seascape below her windows was transformed at twilight by sunsets of tangerine magnificence, and at night it was an ebony mirror that reflected the dazzle of the moon. Edith pronounced herself well content and got back to work. Two days later the *Arcadia* steamed its way out of the harbour and, as Captain Mayne had promised, saluted her by two farewell blasts from the siren. The first half of our journey was over.

The day before we left, I returned from my flying dash across the thousand miles that separated me from my family, to prepare for the press conference. On the appointed day the large room was filled with men and women armed with scribbling blocks, microphones and television cameras. Edith did nothing to disappoint them. She amused them, shocked them, delighted them. Laughter broke from them in tiny explosions round the room and became more sustained as they relaxed. In spite of the fact that no refreshments were offered, when the time came for me to call a halt they were reluctant to go. They saw to it, however, that the Australian public had a chance to get to know her, and their only regret was that she had been unable to get to know them.

Next day we boarded the *Willem Ruys* for the second, ill-fated half of the voyage.

From the beginning, everything went wrong. Edith's and Sister's passports had been packed by mistake and went on board with the luggage. The one bad-mannered press photographer she encountered refused to take no for an answer and photographed her as she was being carried on board by the ambulance men. The cabin, although it was the best that the ship could offer, was poky in comparison with her stateroom. Sister, although I had secured a berth for her next door, had to share quarters with three others. We set out on a sunlit afternoon, but almost at once the seas became tumultuous. New Zealand offered a haven of a few hours only, and the Pacific was so unusually rough that we not only broke a stabiliser, but had to jettison our visit to Pitcairn Island. Women passengers wandered hysterically through the ship, wearing their life-belts and declaring that we would undoubtedly sink. When this was conveyed to Edith she was disapproving.

'Hysteria of any kind', she said, 'should be confined to the housemaid's cupboard.'

None the less, by the time we reached Panama City, she was the colour of her sheets and the shadows under her eyes were blue-black.

The news that she had been made a Companion of Literature cheered her, but not sufficiently to alleviate the nervous fatigue from which she was suffering. Our arrival in Miami brought with it a major disappointment. We had, as I have already said, chosen this route back because of her desire to see her American friends. Unfortunately, Miami was almost as difficult to reach as London Airport. Messages and presents were stacked up ready for her, but there were no friends to welcome her. The sickness that had nothing to do with sea travel, but which accompanied nervous distress, began to manifest itself. I knew, when we docked at Miami, that all was far from well with her, but I was not prepared for the message with which the steward woke me next morning:

'Dame Edith is dangerously ill. Sister says would you please get the priest.'

She had started a haemorrhage during the night, and although the bleeding had stopped she was still very weak. I went in search of a priest, and also spoke to the doctor. His report was more cheerful than I had dared hope, and it was decided that she should remain on board at least as far as Bermuda.

The days that followed were among the worst in my memory. For Sister Farquhar, who carried the burden of responsibility, they must have been agonising. But at least she was in a position to do something for Edith. For me there were only the hours of waiting.

The world of a ship is an enclosed one in which friendships blossom with the suddenness of hot-house flowers and usually die just as quickly when exposed to the outside world. I shall never forget the friends I made on board the *Willem Ruys*, nor the support and consolation they offered me. The purser, a bulky genial Dutchman, proved to be a tower of strength. He arranged for a doctor to come on board at Bermuda for a second opinion. His diagnosis was not reassuring. The haemorrhage could have one of several causes, any of which might prove fatal. On the other hand, it could be due to a varicose vein condition at the base of the throat. In either event she must be taken ashore so that tests could be carried out without delay.

It was raining that day in Bermuda. Edith, her skin the texture as well as the colour of brown paper, was trussed up in blankets and carried on a stretcher to the ferry. Visitors to the ship, fascinated by the unexpected drama, lined the gangway to watch while she was lifted on to the little boat that tossed in the roughened water of the harbour. I went ahead to elbow onlookers out of the way, hating the curiosity that cheapened our anxiety by making it a public thing. In that moment I understood something of the degradation of the limelight that distorts emotion by compelling it to be self-conscious.

I shall never be able to imagine Bermuda as a sunlit holiday resort. For me it is a sombre place with tropical flowers blossoming disconsolately beneath leaden skies, the air smelling of dust dampened by rain, the tawdry buildings mocking my joyless mood with their spatter of paint. The skies had opened when we arrived at the docks and the problem of disembarkation solved by the unorthodox method of lifting her over the side into the outstretched hands of the brown-skinned ambulance men below. Edith's courage, usually so high, quailed before the insecurity of being handled like cargo over the swirling green sea, but, foreseeing what was to happen, I raced ashore through the dockland corridors in time to join the ambulance men. As they reached for her stretcher, I reached for her hand, holding it as strongly as possible until she was safely inside the ambulance. As I did so, I murmured reassurances, willing my vitality into the frail body, which, for the first time in my acquaintance with her, was uttering sounds of fear.

I waited with her until Sister had rejoined us, then put the luggage into a taxi and made my way to the hospital.

There I had to leave her. Someone had to accompany the rest of the luggage back to England, and of the two of us Sister Farquhar was the more necessary to her. The doctor did his best to comfort me. If the tests were favourable, he said, she would be flown home in a matter of days. The whistle blew its warning to passengers ashore as I made my dismal way back to the ship. Ahead of me were five days in which to wonder whether Edith was alive or dead.

Blessedly, the diagnosis of varicose veins proved to be correct. A wire from my good friend Mumper brought the news that Edith had already arrived back at Greenhill. On arrival I marshalled the fifteen pieces of luggage through the hazards of customs and changes of trains from Plymouth to Victoria, and went straight to Hampstead.

I found her pale. She was tired, but she was alive.

Chapter Sixteen

My hangers-on have taught me the meaning of the word immortality.
Edith Sitwell to Timothy Green

BACK IN the comfort of her flat, Edith's spirit reasserted itself. The medical diagnosis of her condition was reassuring. Though she was no better for her voyage, she was no worse. The threat of pneumonia had for the time being been averted and part at least of the object of the voyage had been achieved: she had written the first five chapters of her memoirs.

This was a start and a good one, for she had to fight not only the weakness of her body, but also her reluctance to work; as *The Queens and the Hive* continued to be a best-seller, her incentive to write diminished, and 'My publishers are badgering me to finish that damn book,' became a favourite complaint. She knew that, to maintain her household and pay the doctors' fees, she must continue to make money. The advances offered for her memoirs on both sides of the Atlantic pleased her by establishing her current value as a writer. It was less pleasing, however, that, in taking the lid off the Pandora's box of her life, she released both bitterness and gall. Because of this, she used her book to settle old scores, and in so doing, lessened its impact.

Graham Nicol of Hutchinson continued his Saturday afternoon visits, and I made a point of being there with him so that between us we could make an attempt to establish perspective as well as stimulate her interest. We also provided an audience to whom she could read what she had written during the week. If, because of writer's cramp or some other setback, nothing had been achieved, we questioned her to evoke buried memories, using a tape recorder so that her answers could be typed and presented to her later. Edith was indulgent towards our efforts but totally uninterested in the results. The art of writing for her was the art of presentation of her material. The factual matter on which she drew brought with it the pain of associations. She escaped from it into the portraits which adorn the book and by poking fun at her denigrators. But some of these 'interviews' of ours produced comments that are worth reproducing.

As John Freeman said, she was a difficult, though fascinating, subject for interview because the answers she made were seldom direct.

To the question, for instance, how she would analyse her recognition of genius, she replied that it was 'a kind of smell'.

'Would you say that you always had this?'

'I never had the chance to find out until I came to London.'

'Was there anything in common between, let us say, Dylan Thomas and Tchelitchew, apart from their genius?'

'Oh, I think a great dislike.'

'How would you describe Gertrude Stein, for the benefit of posterity?'

'She was verbally very interesting.'

'And Diaghilev?'

'Terrifying. He used to appear at the ballet with a court of young men behind him. I somehow always managed to find myself with my back to the gentlemen's lavatory, so that nobody could get in or out.'

The subject of H. G. Wells reminded her of his 'wildly funny', though 'very caddish', attack on Henry James.

'He describes a novel written in the Jamesian manner, with a butler called Mortimer and a strange "spirit" that turned out to be a hoard of 1813 brandy. James was furious because he helped H. G. quite a lot.'

'H. G. could be an unpleasant customer then?'

'Oh, perfectly odious. He was to me at one time. I met him at a party afterwards and ignored him. He came up to me and said, "You don't know who I am." I said, "Oh yes I do, Mr Wells, you were extremely rude to me and I saw no reason to recognise you."'

'Was he with his wife or the Baroness?'

'Oh, his wife. In those days I never met anybody who wasn't. I had to have the marriage lines shown to me, so to speak.'

'That must have imposed fairly tight restrictions amongst the people you came up against?'

'Oh, it did. I was once at a party where the only respectable people were myself and the Dolly Sisters.'

Asked about the recent performance of *Façade* she answered that she was very grateful to *The Times* and would never forget their chivalrous apology. 'But,' she said, 'I am a very ferocious old lady, you know, and do not always forgive my enemies. Osbert once told me that an American who had been rude to me was going to have all his teeth out. I said, "Oh, dear! Well, never mind. We must always remember that his teeth will be far better off without him."'

Her letters written at this time show that the 'ferocious old lady' was in fine fighting form once more.

'There is a new terror in Hampstead,' she wrote to Graham Greene. 'A club for the purpose of reciting. They helped themselves (without permission) to my poem "Still Falls the Rain" (which is copyright) and a quantity of them recited this, first doing a twist and then staring out of the window so that the poem is evidently not, as I had thought, a very tragic poem about the bombing of England but an advertisement for mackintoshes! Some people might be rather cross!'

To Jeanne Stonor she wrote that she was 'beating up the press' and that 'the Society of Authors are going to give Sir Allen Lane hell about the near-libel of their latest Penguin, which did not, exactly, do me justice.'

And to me she complained that 'the Oxford University Press—about whom a friend who had better be nameless has said that their activities are one long campaign against the written word—have taken a poem of mine from *Façade* and called it "Long Steel Grass". In fact it is called "Trio for Two Cats and a Trombone". It is about a couple of cats, do you see, having a love affair. It's extremely impertinent of them to have altered it.'

The word 'impertinent' was a favourite missile during

[182]

these last irascible years, hurled usually at the Philistines, and perhaps no word in her vocabulary was more symbolic of the division between her private and public personality. It became an automatic response to sacrilege committed against her public image. In private, I never heard her say to anybody that they were impertinent, but then, in her presence, they never were.

Literary skirmishes had temporarily taken the place of her crusade against cruelty. She wrote to Graham Greene that she was engaged in 'a furious row with a lot of indescribably bad writers. I have told them I have got nothing against them excepting that (a) they have got nothing in their heads; (b) they don't know one word from another; and (c) they can't write.'

She said a great deal more in the *Times Literary Supplement* in a letter defending Laurence Durrell's new P.E.N. anthology. To anybody who knew her during this time, this particular letter conveys a special pathos. Physically weak and dependent on others for her survival, her proud spirit clung to a conception of the literary lioness who could still terrify and subdue. She was aware of the fact that her weapons had lost the cutting edge that made them formidable earlier in her life but attempted to compensate for them by her fame and by the threat of her coming book.

This was the letter:

Sir,

Mr Laurence Durrell, who is the editor of the new P.E.N. anthology, is in trouble with the reviewer of that book because he is a fine writer and therefore famous.

I do not know from under what dull meaningless stone the writer of that review crawled! But I understand that persons of that kind think I am laughing at them! . . . Were I not too kind to laugh at the cruel disappointment and envy suffered by poor unsuccessful little people of this kind, I might be amused by the fact that although I am now 76 years of age, the unsuccessful are still thrown into what is practically an epileptic fit brought on by envy and malice at the mere mention of my name! . . . Perhaps they would like *me* to take notice of them. In any case whether they would, or would not like it, I am going to do it in my forthcoming book.

This evoked from the reviewer, Nicholas Newton, the reply that he was 'puzzled by Dame Edith Sitwell's reference to the "dull meaningless stone" from under which your reviewer allegedly crawled. Since she introduced the stone, surely it's her responsibility to give it a meaning.'

Her answer was dismissive:

Sir,

I always read your correspondence columns with a varying degree of interest but I am a little anxious this week about a letter from a Mr Nicholas Newton.

Do you think it is safe to allow him to go out alone?

I am sorry I have not the time in which to explain to Mr Newton what a stone is (he has probably never heard of sculptors and architects). He should consult a geologist.

Mr Newton ended the exchange with the comment he was 'touched by Dame Edith Sitwell's thoughtful letter, but still unsatisfied. I asked for bread and received a stone.'

Robert Conquest muscled in to the fight with a poem beginning:

> If you must print a review
> With cracks about Dame Edith, you
> Will find the lady's cries of vengeance
> Ring louder, far, than those of ten gents.'

It continued on this level for another thirty lines or so. Edith's reply was more in her old style:

Sir,

It was very nice to see R. Conquest's nice long letter in your correspondence columns. I always knew he had it in him.

What came to be known as the 'Ugh' correspondence resulted from a review of *Dead Fingers Talk*, written by William Burroughs and published by John Calder. During her stay in Sydney, Edith had received a volume of plays edited by John Calder which she described as written with 'indescribable obscenity'. This kind of literature offended her sensibilities on aesthetic rather than moral grounds, but she was incensed enough by it to send it off to the office of the Public Prosecutor. The advice she received was that to prosecute such a publication would be to draw attention to it. She saw the sense of this and abandoned the project, though with reluctance. When *Dead Fingers Talk* was reviewed in the *Times Literary Supplement* under the exclamation 'Ugh' she picked up her pen.

Sir,
    I was delighted to see in your issue of the 14th inst. the very right-minded review of a novel by Mr Burroughs (whoever he may be) published by a Mr John Calder (whoever he may be).
    The public canonisation of that insignificant, dirty little book, *Lady Chatterley's Lover*, was a signal to persons who wish to unload the filth in their minds on the British public.
    As the author of *Gold Coast Customs*, I can scarcely be accused of shirking reality, but I do not wish to spend the rest of my life with my nose nailed to other people's lavatories.
    I prefer Chanel No. 5.

That she enjoyed her campaign by correspondence goes without saying, and she used it to provide an outlet for the frustrations of illness and old age. What she needed was a new interest.

Once again it was provided by a musician.

Malcolm Williamson, the young Australian composer, fresh from his successful setting of Graham Greene's *Our Man in Havana*, came to see her with the request that he might use her *English Eccentrics* as the basis for an opera which had been commissioned by Benjamin Britten for the Aldeburgh Festival. Geoffrey Dunn was to write the libretto, and Robert Helpmann, it was hoped, was to produce.

Edith was delighted. In due course Geoffrey Dunn

appeared to read part one of his libretto. His skill in adapting her text assured Edith's co-operation and the next time he came he was with Robert Helpmann, the third member of the trio.

Robert Helpmann, who, Edith said, was the best mimic she knew, sat with the others beside her bed and lived up to his reputation by telling her story after story. Edith laughed until the tears ran down her face, begging him to repeat her favourites for our benefit. With his volatile, young-old face, illumined by large expressive eyes, his slight body electric with vitality, and his movements controlled as only a dancer's can be, he looked like a graceful mixture of a pekinese and a wasp. The stories he told were mainly of the theatre, but there was one that has stayed in my memory because it happened at Renishaw, to which he had been invited for the weekend.

The house-party had decided to dress up for the benefit of Somerset Maugham, who had been invited to dinner. After lunch Robert Helpmann stayed in the house, planning his costume, and at the appointed time swept down the stairs, dressed as Queen Alexandra, to greet the new arrival. When he got there he found that the others had decided to abandon the idea, and were all in ordinary clothes. Somerset Maugham, he said, shook hands without comment.

Malcolm Williamson, Robert Helpmann and myself being Australians, the conversation touched on the difficulties of Australians living abroad. Malcolm Williamson voiced one of the minor puzzles presented by English titles; for instance, there might be a Lady Mary Smith, but there might also be a Mary, Lady Smith.

The christian name before the title indicated a dowager, Edith explained.

'But Tennyson was always known as Alfred, Lord Tennyson,' Malcolm objected.

'Ah, but then he *was* a dowager,' Edith said promptly.

These days, Edith remained in bed. Only for a large party did she consent to get up, and then it was most unwillingly. The friends who continued to appear two or three times a week became used to sipping their drinks around the large bed with Edith lying flat on her back, her head on the pillows, her baby fluff of brown hair, in which there was still no trace of grey, brushed back from the wide forehead.

This supine position gave rise to anxiety. Sister Farquhar did her best to support her by massing pillows behind her; Jeanne Stonor, one of the most constant and practical of her visitors, warned of the danger to the lungs; her doctor of the moment rigged up a contraption by which she could pull herself up. Edith, whose wrists were too delicate and whose muscles were too atrophied to make use of it, consented to her daily treatment by the physiotherapist and lapsed back on her bed. It was an uphill fight that was lost on the day after Sister Farquhar took a well-deserved holiday in the autumn of that year, 1963.

A relief nurse had been established, and I came in early in the afternoon to make sure that all was well. I found Edith lying with her knees higher than her head, her colour high, her breathing ominously shallow. When I described to the doctor her difficulties in articulation, a cerebral haemorrhage was suspected, but in fact it was pneumonia. By the time she left for the hospital she was too delirious to recognise me.

It was the second of her major crises of health. Her family were informed by telephone that she had a fifty-fifty chance of survival. For the first of many such nights, I slept with the extension of my telephone switched through to my bedside. Morning dawned without news, but by next day she was considered to have passed the crisis. A few days later I received a reassuringly irritable phone call from her, asking that I bring in a present for her nurse and some decent wine to make the hospital food bearable. A fortnight later she was back at Greenhill.

She had scarcely been back a month when a telegram arrived from Paris informing us that Evelyn Wiel had broken her hip and been taken to hospital where she must remain for the rest of her life. We kept the news from Edith as long as we could; then, a week before Christmas we broke it to her. And in consequence, early in the morning of a foggy Boxing Day, I set off once more for Paris.

The reason for my journey was not entirely Edith's anxiety on behalf of her old friend. That she remained fond of Evelyn Wiel was, in view of the drain she represented on her finances, a proof of loyalty. She was determined that the allowance she sent to Evelyn each month should continue, but she was equally determined not to be held responsible for hospital fees that might continue indefinitely. I went to Paris to make this clear to the authorities and to remove the last of Edith's possessions from the flat at 129 rue St Dominique.

I did not look forward to the task ahead of me. My sympathies, as well as my loyalty, were with Edith; to her Helen Rootham's eight-year-long illness and her sister's twenty-five-year-long dependence appeared in retrospect as the shackling of a life-time, and her resentment was sharpened by infirmity. Yet I could not help feeling sad for Evelyn, now over eighty and senile. To be confined to hospital for the rest of her days was an unhappy fate for this gallant, though mercenary, old woman.

At the hospital the almoner was sympathetic and the matron belonged among those dedicated women in whose hands the least deserving of us are safe. I saw to the necessary financial adjustments, made sure that everything was being done for Evelyn that could be done and made my way back to the rue St Dominique.

Here I was confronted with a problem. Short of breaking open the door I had no way of getting in. There had been no sign of a key at the hospital and Evelyn had not been lucid enough to tell me where to find one.

Fortunately, I remembered her mentioning a neighbour who came in to cook for her. There was only one adjoining flat on the fifth floor. I took a chance and rang the doorbell. It opened and Madame Ottolard appeared.

A tiny, volatile French widow, she had been the prop on whom Evelyn had leaned for some years. I managed to convey to her that I had come in search of Edith's possessions, and suggested that there might be more paintings hidden away somewhere, perhaps even a portrait of Dame Edith.

Madame Ottolard put her bird-like head on one side and looked thoughtful, then motioned me towards the tiny room that had been Edith's bedroom. The shutters were closed, one central naked bulb threw a yellow light on the piles of dusty books, the bare boards, the crumbling furniture. Against one wall was a heavy old bookcase of Victorian vintage. I indicated that the search might begin behind this and together we tugged at it, managing finally to get it away from the wall.

There, behind the bookcase, we found our cache of treasure—a dozen or so of Tchelitchew ink drawings and a portrait of Edith.

As soon as I saw it, I was conscious of excitement. I shook Madame Ottolard by the hand.

'It's good,' I told her. 'It's very good!'

It was a crayon in profile of Edith's head and shoulders. The long blond hair fell beside the delicate nose that dominated the small Tudor mouth and the regressive chin. The mauve dress she wore moulded the curve of neck and shoulders. In that dim and dusty light it seemed to belong more to the Renaissance than to this century. It was unlike any other of the portraits by Tchelitchew. Spots of mould, later removed, bore witness to its years of incarceration.

Much encouraged, I went back into the little room. While we had been pulling at the bookcase I had noticed a line extending from a hole in the wallpaper behind it. It might have been a crack but it looked rather too even for that. I put the tip of a pencil into the hole and turned to Madame Ottolard with fresh excitement. Was there, perhaps, another key to be found somewhere in the flat?

Madame Ottolard looked doubtful but was obliging. A few minutes later she returned, brandishing a large and rusty key which we inserted into the hole. It fitted. The wallpaper came away with a shower of plaster and the door of a cupboard that had been papered over swung out.

At first sight the contents were a disappointment. There were various odds and ends of no value, one or two books, a broken sun umbrella, some glass ornaments, all covered in black dust. Then I saw a pile of stiff-covered notebooks neatly piled in one corner. I opened one and felt the thrill of discovery. It was the original manuscript of *I Live Under a Black Sun*. I went through the others. There were fifty-six notebooks in all, and in them were Edith's complete prose works written during her period in France.

That night I telephoned London and next day I set off with my booty in the back of the car. Edith had been ill with worry, but my news had restored her spirits. From then on except for a period during which it was sent to a Tchelitchew exhibition in New York, the portrait did not leave her sight. The pleasure it brought her was my reward. The manuscript books were put into a sale and realised three thousand pounds.

The last and most fruitful of my treasure hunts to the rue St Dominique was accomplished.

Chapter Seventeen

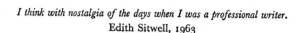

I think with nostalgia of the days when I was a professional writer.
Edith Sitwell, 1963

BED-RIDDEN, with an infected finger that curtailed her ability to write, Edith's main pleasure now consisted in entertaining her family and her friends. To do this in comfort she needed more space. The four cats, her solace and delight, had wrought havoc in the flat, and the noise, always an irritation, seemed to have reached a new crescendo. It was obvious that better accommodation must be found.

The problem was to find it in the centre of London, to which her family wanted her to move.

'*Four* cats, madam? Oh no, I'm afraid not.'

I became used to the tone of voice which accompanied the words.

'Two, perhaps?' one agent suggested hopefully, as though the disposal of two cats was a minor matter.

In the meantime Edith became interested in a fresh controversy. Her old friend A. L. Rowse had produced a new book on Shakespeare and Edith was in amicable but adamant disagreement with his theories.

'I wish they would leave the old gentleman alone,' she observed. 'I wrote to Alec Guinness this morning and told him that I simply do not dare to open the morning papers in case I find that Enid Blyton was the real author of *King Lear*. I like Mr Rowse, who has always been charming to me, but between ourselves he has earls on the brain. The Dark Lady was definitely *not* a friend of Lady Southampton.'

A forthcoming B.B.C memorial to Dylan Thomas brought

a visit from Wynford Vaughan Thomas, but a similar approach from an unknown television producer was refused with the irritable comment: 'I do wish people would stop mountaineering and using me as their alpenstock.'

The trouble was, Edith was bored. Since her reading was curtailed by tired eye-muscles and her writing by the infected finger, her days were long. The infection, a legacy from pneumonia, caused her a great deal of pain and lowered her morale. Her hands being her greatest vanity, to be forced to wear an unsightly bandage upset her.

The reviews of *Music and Ceremonies*, the American edition of her last book of poems, acted as a temporary boost to her morale. 'A short book,' said one, 'but of such magnitude that it must be considered as one of the major books of poetry by a living poet.' 'Her words are the perfectly controlled, powerful and intense expression of a poetic sensibility which has a grandeur and a vigour found in few of today's poets,' said another.

Reports of the Tchelitchew exhibition in New York pleased her even more. Monroe Wheeler wrote to say, 'To almost everybody's astonishment the show appears to be having an extraordinary popular success. . . . Everybody thinks your portrait is the finest; and the profile in wax is as moving as something from the archaeology of Ur.'

'Poor boy,' she said to me. 'If only he had had some of that success when he needed it.'

She asked me to arrange for all the press cuttings concerning the exhibition to be sent to her, and was moved to the same fury by the one negative review she read as she would have been if it had been directed against herself or her brothers.

'I'm going to write and tell the little pets that great artists are used to expectorations from the gutter,' she said.

A counter-irritant was always an effective antidote to boredom as far as Edith was concerned, but, the letter written, the problem of inactivity remained. With it came the increasing burden of the memoirs.

The work she had done on them since her return had been sporadic. The book was still in pieces and she was no longer capable of pulling it into shape. But there was no turning back. The American and the English advances had already been paid in part. I knew there was only one thing to do and, as soon as I could, I did it. Gathering up as much of her material as I could lay my hands on, I got to work with scissors and paste. It was the greatest compliment that she ever paid me that she let me do it for her. The results could not be compared with the book she would have produced if her health had been better, but at least there was a book, and she was able to check it herself. By the end of the month, it was ready for the agents.

My work on the memoirs led to a further method of interesting her that would make no demands on her strength.

I had always thought that Edith was a great prose writer, but my researches during this time showed me that she was also a very witty journalist. It seemed to me that an anthology compiled from her articles, reviews, lectures, broadcasts and books, would make the kind of bedside companion that I, for one, would like to possess. The idea pleased her, and it was agreed that the collecting of the material would be my part of the project. For Edith would remain only the selection— a task designed to stimulate rather than to drain her resources.

Hutchinson expressed interest in publishing it and work was begun, though never completed. It cannot be claimed that the task solved the difficulties of the last year of her life, but there is no doubt that it fulfilled its purpose at the time.

In May of 1964 my house-hunting, which had turned to the Hampstead area, bore fruit. A cottage came up for rent in Keats Grove.

As soon as I saw the tiny Queen Anne house opposite Keats' former home, with creepers luxuriating beside the blue painted door and the large room overlooking the minute but brilliant splash of garden at the back, I knew that I had found what I was looking for. Its assets were many: a patio for the cats, tasteful furniture, burglar-proof windows, a landlady who was an animal-lover, not to mention the all-important fact that I would still be within easy reach in an emergency.

I did not need the genial salesmanship of Mr Donovan of Potters to convince me that it was a find. I drove back to

Greenhill and scooped up Sister Farquhar so that she could see it. She, too, fell in love with it at first sight. So also did Edith when, a month later, she made the move, 'I long to show you and Barbara the house and garden (found for me by my dear Elizabeth),' she wrote to Henry Cecil, 'both of which are really very pretty.'

The family pronounced official approval and the cottage was named 'Bryher House' as a gesture of gratitude to the friend who had helped her so much when she needed it. But this was not until she had returned from her holiday at Bournemouth.

Of all the decisions with which Edith continued to surprise me, this trip was, I think, the most unexpected.

The reason for it was that Sister, remembering the crisis that had arisen during her absence the previous year, was reluctant to leave Edith again; whereas Edith was adamant that 'the poor girl must have a holiday'. In any case, she said, the choice between Bournemouth and a relief nurse was one between two evils. The kind, boring creature who had been installed on that never-to-be-forgotten occasion had left an indelible memory of 'non-stop conversation about the kitchen sink and where she should put the saucepans. I felt as though I had been incarcerated in a play by Mr Osborne or Miss Delaney'.

So to Bournemouth they went, to a hotel that had the double advantage of being familiar and quiet (boasting that the Beatles had hidden there for a week's rest). I stayed behind to organise the move to Keats Grove, and by the time Edith got back all was ready for her. Her books, gathered from Renishaw, Paris and Greenhill, graced shelves that had been specially built for them. Her third folio Shakespeare was housed in a glass cabinet in the hall. Her Tchelitchews were distributed on the walls, and opposite her bed was the portrait I had found in Paris. The one hazard that we had feared—the narrow little flight of stairs leading to her bedroom—was manoeuvred in safety. The cats bounded joyously over the canvas-covered furniture into the patio at the back. All was well at Bryher House.

But all was not well with Edith. Shortly after her arrival a lassitude overcame her. At first we put it down to fatigue from the journey to and from Bournemouth, but as time went on it became obvious that there was more to it than that. She began to sleep through her days. When she woke, her speech was vague. A short conversation was enough to tire her and her visitors had the disconcerting experience of watching her eyes close as they conversed with her. To talk work or business, to ask her for decisions, even on simple household matters, became impossible. Not even her cats could rouse her from her torpor.

I cast around for a new stimulus and found one through John Downing, an actor and a friend of us both. He offered to come each day and read to her. It was a sign of her state of health that, in spite of her public statement that she would want to kill anybody who read aloud to her, she agreed to this with every sign of pleasure.

Looking back over those anxious months, it is pleasant to think of the sunlit mornings when Edith lay on her large bed with its saffron cover, listening to her own early writings to the accompaniment of birds serenading her from the trees outside her window. John Downing read her the memoirs and he read her the prose pieces. To increase his audience she insisted that Sister be there as well and, when something especially delighted her, it must be read again to me when I arrived.

In the years that I had been with her, many young men had served her not only because of their admiration and affection, but because of the fascination she exerted over them. They included Gordon Watson, Michael Stapleton, Alberto de Lacerda and Malcolm Williamson. John Downing was the last of them and the only one among us in this difficult time who was able to bring her certain pleasure.

Those autumn months of 1964 were unhappy ones. Tensions arose among us. Anxiety for Edith's health, responsibilities that had become a burden, brought an edge to the relationships of those whose concern was to do their best for her. The contradictions of her nature, emphasised by weakness, the suspicions of the outside world, barred from access to her by medical restrictions, caused misunderstandings and hurt feelings. Years of experience had taught me to decode her true motives and her true wishes from what she said and did not say. Few among the rest of her circle had had time enough to learn the code. Like all people who are old and ill she tended to look for a focus for her misery and complain about one to the other. The fact that her household was not completely divided against itself is a proof of the devotion she inspired.

In the midst of the half-world between sleeping and waking, she was visited by her old friend and fellow poet, Marianne Moore. A tiny woman in a wide straw hat, she, too, was suffering from the after-effects of illness, and their encounter had an element of the macabre in it. They conversed, these women of great talent who were bound by genuine affection, but their conversation reached out and never quite made a connection. The little bird-like woman fluttered away, leaving a trail of disconnected sentences behind her, and Edith closed her eyes and returned to sleep.

The London opening of *English Eccentrics* loomed ahead. Michael Stapleton and I had reported back on the Aldeburgh performance with such enthusiasm that Edith was determined to be present. So weak that the least strain reduced her to tears, scarcely able to sit up in her wheelchair, she appeared that night by will-power alone. This time there was no new hat, no magnificent costume. She looked what was she was, a frail old woman, alive because of the spirit by which she lived, and present because of the stimulus offered by an opera that must have been similar to the one discussed by Tchelitchew and herself all those years ago.

Malcolm Williamson alone came back to receive her congratulations after the performance, and when a few days later, a party for the cast was planned, she was unable to be present.

At our wits' end, Sister and I had further consultations with her family, with the result that yet another doctor appeared at Bryher House. With him, miraculously, came a temporary recovery. The changes he insisted on were taxing but effective, and for a short time she seemed to return to her old self. The torpor went, leaving a deposit of energy which she used to 'practise verse technique', as she put it to Jeanne Stonor. But 'the poisoning in my left hand has now spread to my right and the doctors say I am to use my hands as little as possible,' she reported to me.

Reading became a possibility once more, and for a while it seemed that Edith was almost herself again; almost but not quite. The last round in a 'grand row' she had been having with Julian Symons took the form of an article he had written for *London Magazine*, a carefully documented attempt to demolish her reputation with the purpose, the editor told her, of starting a Sitwellian controversy. It came too late. The lioness reacted with a fierce enough show of claws, but illness prevented her from using them. It was left to her friends to champion her cause. John Lehmann wrote an answer to the magazine and Henry Cecil—amongst many others—wrote to her with such warmth that she was reassured. 'How unfailingly good you and Barbara are to me. Your kindness in giving up part of your time—you who are the busiest of men and can hardly have a moment for yourself—to write me that comforting and most amusing letter is so great. It made me feel much better,' she wrote.

Nevertheless, her fighting spirit was far from subdued.

'I do not take the outpourings of these planet microbes— as Hitler called the inhabitants of the globe—very seriously,' she informed the friends who sympathised with her. A letter written to Graham Greene, dated December 1st, is very much in her old style. It begins with an apology for her delay in writing to him, explaining: 'I have been in agonising pain from a "bug" caught in that infernal hospital in which I was incarcerated with pneumonia. I ought, of course, to be very grateful to them for not blinding me, which they do in some hospitals now. . . .

'Jeanne says you are in torture with sciatica. It is *hell*—as I know, having been the Sciatica Queen while in Hollywood. Let me advise you; the only thing which helps the pain is aspirin. I used to have eight aspirin tablets in twenty-four hours. That and Bengue's Balsam not rubbed but spread on. . . .

'Here comes one of my cats who has just had an accident, poor boy. He is guiding my pen.'

From this it can be seen that, a week before her death, Edith was still very much alive.

At about the time she wrote this letter, John and Catherine Freeman came in to see her with the news of the Tchelitchew exhibition which John had visited in New York in company with Bette Davis, the film actress. They had both, he told her, decided that the portrait found in Paris was the best thing in it. Edith was delighted and regaled them with the scandalous stories she loved to tell. They went away with the promise of a visit the following week.

Her agents were now able to talk business once more. David Higham came in to discuss the prose pieces, Jean LeRoy to receive Edith's thanks for the news of generous serial rights for the memoirs sold to the *Sunday Times*. She began to plan the party she would give when the book came out.

As I arrived at the blue door on the evening of December 8th things seemed, at long last, to have returned to normal.

PART III

The End

Chapter Eighteen

. . . An overtone
From some lonely world unknown.
'Aubade'

THERE HAD been, as Edith herself might have said, 'signs and portents'.

Months beforehand, one day when I came in to see her, she had greeted me with the news that she had written the last line for her memoirs:

'It's all over now bar the shouting and the worms.'

She looked at me as she spoke, her eyes filled with a pre-science that robbed me of speech. She then wrote out the last paragraph of the book, and gave it to Graham Nicol to be added in proof.

A month or so later, a friend of ours with what is known as 'extra-sensory perception' came to me in a state of near hysteria. He was experiencing manifestations of blood. They had appeared on his shirt, on the carpet of his bedroom, in the wash basin.

'You know the cause,' he said.

I said that I did not.

'Edith.'

For her birthday, she had received a particularly beautiful bouquet of white orchids from a friend who, years before, had read her horoscope. For some reason the bouquet was never acknowledged and the friend rang me to find out if they had arrived.

'How is Dame Edith?' she asked.

I replied that she was a great deal better, although the last two years had not been good ones as far as her health was concerned. She answered that Edith's horoscope had been shadowed during this time. 'But,' she added, 'she won't die until her work is finished.'

A sceptic by nature, I dismissed these words as I had dismissed the 'manifestations'.

On the night of December 8th, as I waited outside her house for Sister to let me in, I had no premonition of any kind. Graham Nicol arrived shortly after I did, bringing the illustrations from which she was to make her choice for the memoirs and the photographer, Paula Davies, who was to photograph the Tchelitchew portrait that I had discovered in Paris. Sister remained downstairs to help with this, while Graham and I went up to see Edith.

She was rather more irritable than usual, casting out one or two of the family photographs because she did not want her parents 'muscling in on the book'. But this was nothing unusual. She loved to outrage us, and by the time she had finished, she was laughing with us.

We got up to go. 'Well, Edith,' Graham said. 'It won't be long now before I bring you the proofs. Your work on the book is finished.'

'Thank the Lord for that,' she said.

We were laughing as we left her. That night I went out to dinner and returned to my flat at about midnight. When I got back I found a message for me to ring Sister.

Edith had been haemorrhaging again. Would I please get the doctor at once: she had been trying to get through to him without success. I did what she asked and then got back into my car and returned to Bryher House. We decided not to let Edith know I was there, as we did not want to alarm her, and I waited downstairs until the doctor came. After he had seen her he sent me home. There was no need to notify the family yet.

It was then four-thirty in the morning. I went back to my flat, though not to sleep. At a quarter to eight Sister rang again. Edith was being taken to hospital for a blood transfusion. Would I please inform the family while she rang for the ambulance? I put in a call to Sacheverell and Georgia Sitwell and then, once again, hurried round to Bryher House.

The ambulance had arrived by the time I got there, and

Edith was already on her stretcher. Her face was the colour and the texture of brown paper, as it had been in Bermuda.

'Oh, Elizabeth, I have had such an awful night,' she said to me.

I put my cheek against hers, refraining from telling her that I had been there with her. The ambulance men lifted her gently.

'I'm afraid I'm being an awful nuisance,' Edith apologised.

I went down the stairs behind them as she left Bryher House for the last time and watched while she was trussed up in the ambulance with Sister beside her.

'I'll see you very soon,' I said and kissed my hand to her as I always did when I said goodbye. She managed to pull one hand out of the blankets to kiss it back to me. That was my last sight of her.

I did my best to busy myself with her affairs, waiting for the telephone. At midday there was still hope. Then I received two phone calls, the first from Francis and the second from Reresby Sitwell. The tears in Reresby's voice told me what I dreaded to hear. Edith was sinking fast. I rang for a taxi and went downstairs to be ready for it. I gave the address of the hospital to the driver.

'And please hurry,' I added.

He was truculent. 'Everybody always wants to hurry in the rush hour,' he said.

I did not reply. I remember marvelling at such a response when I had asked for a hospital, but my whole being was concentrated on the battle being fought in that hospital room on the other side of London.

Every car in London seemed to be part of a conspiracy to block our progress. Then, about five minutes before we arrived, I was conscious of a release of tension. My spirits lifted. I felt oddly peaceful in the back of that crawling taxi.

We pulled up outside the waiting room. The driver's tone was menacing:

'It's over the five-mile limit. I'll settle for a quid.'

I gave him the pound without looking at him. Through

the open door I could see Sister Farquhar. She was sitting alone and her expression was sufficient to tell me the news.

'When did it happen?' I asked.

'About five minutes ago,' she said.

Index